SOCIAL RESPONSIBILITY and ENVIRONMENTAL SUSTAINABILITY in BUSINESS

SOCIAL RESPONSIBILITY and ENVIRONMENTAL SUSTAINABILITY in BUSINESS

How Organizations Handle Profits and Social Duties

Edited by

Preeta M. Banerjee
Vanita Shastri

Response
Business books from SAGE
Los Angeles ▪ London ▪ New Delhi ▪ Singapore ▪ Washington DC
www.sagepublications.com

First published in 2010 by

 **Response Books**
Business books from SAGE
B1/I-1 Mohan Cooperative Industrial Area
Mathura Road, New Delhi 110 044, India

SAGE Publications Inc
2455 Teller Road
Thousand Oaks, California 91320, USA

SAGE Publications Ltd
1 Oliver's Yard, 55 City Road
London EC1Y 1SP, United Kingdom

SAGE Publications Asia-Pacific Pte Ltd
33 Pekin Street
#02-01 Far East Square
Singapore 048763

Second Printing 2012

Published by Vivek Mehra for SAGE Publications India Pvt Ltd, typeset in 11/13pt Minion by Star Compugraphics Private Limited, Delhi and printed at Chaman Enterprises, New Delhi.

Library of Congress Cataloging-in-Publication Data

Social responsibility and environmental sustainability in business: how organizations handle profits and social duties/edited by Preeta M. Banerjee, Vanita Shastri.
    p. cm.
    Includes bibliographical references and index.
    1. Social responsibility of business. 2. Social entrepreneurship. 3. Corporations—Environmental aspects. I. Banerjee, Preeta M. II. Shastri, Vanita.

HD60.S62   658.4'08—dc22   2010   2010027732

ISBN: 978-81-321-0464-3 (PB)

The SAGE Team: Reema Singhal, Anupam Choudhury and Vijay Sah

This book is dedicated to the committed individuals
who work endlessly to promote social good
and the welfare of mankind

Contents

List of Figures

Foreword

Inspiring People to Engage in Social Entrepreneurship

The time is right for entrepreneurs to aim high and step in to solve social challenges innovatively and inexpensively, customizing their solutions to local conditions. As the global economy shrinks and the government and the private sector cut back on spending for social programs, the need to address these pressing social issues becomes more urgent. This is an opportunity for social entrepreneurs to build new models of sustainable growth, to help scale existing solutions, and to create new public–private partnerships. We hope as The Indus Entrepreneurs (TiE) and its members' involvement in this sector grows, its global membership can leverage its expertise and global networks to help build bridges between the haves and the have-nots.

This book addresses this need and the move of social change from corporations to global social entrepreneurs. The authors of this book have social change in common—and also belong to TiE-Boston, the social entrepreneurship special interest group (SIG).

The social entrepreneurship SIG rose out of TiE's annual conference (TiECON) in 2004. TiECON East, the annual conference of TiE-Boston, and one of the largest gatherings of entrepreneurs on the East Coast, attracts hundreds of professionals from diverse walks of life to meet and discuss entrepreneurship. Among the hustle and flow of the technical professionals at TiECON East 2004 in Boston, a new idea was about to be launched. Standing apart from the panels on technical and business topics was a session titled "Doing Well by Doing Good: High Performance Social Entrepreneurs," with a panel of leaders in this field, including David Bornstein, author of the seminal book *How to Change the World: Social Entrepreneurs and the Power of New Ideas* (Bornstein, 2007), and Sonal Shah, founder of Indicorps, a service agency getting young people to commit to a year of service in rural India. With over 300 attendees, the response to the session was overwhelming.

Inspired by the success of the panel, two TiE members, Raj Melville and Deepak Verma, drawn to the idea of channeling the resources and energies of business professionals and entrepreneurs to support and nurture the social sector, began to meet to discuss how the momentum and interest could be best harnessed. Meanwhile, Jugnu Jain, also a TiE-Boston member who was organizing life sciences and health care events at TiE-Boston, was interacting with not-for-profit groups in 2005, such as Institute for One World Health and A Leg to Stand On. These were clearly entrepreneurial organizations but had not been a part of TiE-Boston due to their not-for-profit nature. As she lobbied TiE-Boston to initiate a social entrepreneur (SE) special interest group, she became aware of Raj and Deepak's groundwork.

The two groups joined forces in 2005 and recruited Kris Joshi and Rakesh Pandey to form the core SE team. With the support of the then TiE-Boston President Vinit Nijhawan, the core team conducted a survey of the TiE members to determine the degree of interest in creating a group to support social entrepreneurs. Over a hundred members responded, strongly supporting the concept and indicating their interest in participating. It was exciting to learn that most members were looking to meet people with similar interests, to learn about high-performance social entrepreneurs, and were willing to volunteer and provide mentoring to aspiring social entrepreneurs. Over two-thirds of the members said they were willing to contribute their time or expertise; others were willing to share their networking contacts. The survey also provided guidance on the key areas that captured the attention of most members: sustainable development, education, public health, and microfinance/developmental finance. The primary objective of the group was not fundraising, but exposing the members to quality social impact organizations spanning these four areas, to encourage organizations to share their best practices in panel discussion settings, and to encourage members to volunteer their time and skills.

With this data in hand, the core team launched the SE Group of TiE-Boston with a standing-room-only panel discussion on "International Applications of Microfinance" on April 20, 2006. Working in conjunction with the Grameen Foundation, the panel consisted of an international cross-section of practitioners from India, Morocco, and Pakistan. The discussion opened the eyes of many members to the great strides that microfinance had made and was a predictor of the global focus that microfinance would command when Professor Muhammad Yunus, founder of Grameen Bank, won the Nobel Peace Prize later that year.

The second event in July 2006 focused on education. It featured different models of primary education ranging from informal education to construction worker children (Pratham), one-teacher schools (Ekal Vidyalaya) to inexpensive computers (One Laptop per Child). Over 100 people participated, many of them new to TiE.

Though the SE Group started out with separate groups focused on the main themes identified in the surveys, it was soon apparent that members' interests and social entrepreneurs themselves spanned several areas. So it made sense to have just one common focus, on social entrepreneurship, for the group.

Building on these early successes and lessons learnt, TiE-Boston SE Group has held nearly two dozen events ranging from intimate dinners with visiting NGO leaders to an annual conference, ForSE: Forum for Social Entrepreneurs, which attracts several hundred aspiring social entrepreneurs and supporters. A selection of organizations and speakers that have been part of these sessions include:

- Royston Braganza, CEO, Grameen Capital
- Gerald Chertavian, founder and CEO, Year Up
- Desh Deshpande, co-founder, Sycamore, founder, Deshpande Foundation

- Amy Smith, MacArthur Fellow, MIT
- Bhuwan Ribhu, founder, Save the Childhood Foundation
- Lisa Nitze, VP, Global Engagement, Ashoka
- Vanessa Kirsch, founder and president, New Profit
- Veena Mankar, founder, CEO, and director, Swadhaar microfinance
- Vikram Sheel Kumar, co-founder, Dimagi
- Iqbal Quadir, founder, Grameen Phone, director, MIT Legatum Center
- Harish Hande, founder, Solar Electric Light Company (SELCO)

With the intense interest in social enterprise, the group has grown over time and now includes over 800 people on its mailing list. The group has created an operational structure that has served it well. The SE Group's mission is to create a forum for social, business, and technical entrepreneurs with a strong interest in social impact. The group facilitates the translation of that interest into action by

- exposing and engaging members in opportunities with leading organizations in the SE arena,
- mentoring emerging SE organizations, and
- building bridges with social entrepreneurs in other communities and geographies.

To help manage the activities of the group and to encourage mentorship, the group has a standing Steering Committee that meets on the second Tuesday of every month. At these meetings:

- Social entrepreneurs looking for help are invited to make 10-minute pitches to the Steering Committee. One of the committee members takes responsibility as the point of contact and facilitates introductions or other resource connections.
- Individual members offer to guide early-stage social entrepreneurs upon request.
- Members help plan out events for the year, help organize sessions and find speakers/panelists.

The current (2009) co-chairs of the SE Group are Ranjani Saigal, Andrew K. Stein, Vithal Deshpande, and Manu Gossain.

When Professor Muhammad Yunus won the Nobel Peace Prize, he instantly increased the profile of social entrepreneurs and social entrepreneurship. With its increasing popularity, the definition of SE has become all encompassing, such that many things fit under the umbrella. Social entrepreneurship oftentimes describes activities that cover the spectrum from traditional non-profits and citizens groups to that of many working within corporations and even the government to address issues in the social sector. More recently, this definition has widened further to include efforts to address environmental and sustainability initiatives as well. While this book addresses the range of options under this definition, the TiE-Boston SE Group chose to focus primarily on entrepreneurs—both from the non-profit and for-profit world—who are working to address a social issue in a sustainable and scalable manner.

The true impact of the SE Group has been in guiding growing social entrepreneurs as they chart their course. Over the past three years, the group has reviewed and mentored over two dozen organizations that have presented at their Steering Committee meetings. Some of the innovative start-ups that have resulted include:

- **Saaf Water:** Saaf Water is a for-profit SE whose mission is to provide affordable clean water to the urban poor in developing countries. Sarah Bird, founder and CEO, defines success as "having a visible social impact and developing a profitable, sustainable enterprise." Sarah leveraged TiE resources in multiple ways in the initial phase of starting SaafWater. Raj Melville, TiE-Boston charter member, assisted Sarah on the initial business plan concept including developing the name SaafWater. With Raj and others' help, SaafWater was a finalist in the MIT 100K Entrepreneurship Competition which provided the seed capital to get Sarah's idea moving. This initial association with TiE led Sarah to more TiE events. At a TiE SE event on microfinance, she was able to connect with the Kashf Foundation, a large microfinance organization in Pakistan. As an attendee at ForSE: Forum for Social Entrepreneurs, Sarah connected with others in the social enterprise community to share experiences and learn valuable insights that helped SaafWater prepare for the challenges of running a social enterprise. (http://www.saafwater.com)

- **Unite for Health:** Unite for Health is a non-profit organization committed to bridging the gap that divides rich and poor countries in disability and death from cardiovascular diseases (like heart attacks or strokes). The organization is developing a simplified but effective guideline for treating cardiovascular disease (CVD) in primary care settings in China. This novel approach is based around a polypill that combines four essential medications for CVD into one pill that could decrease deaths from heart disease by 50 percent for 10 cents a day. This year a pilot work in community health centers in rural and urban areas of China was completed. It was found that current quality of care for heart disease and stroke is poor but could be greatly improved, and that Chinese physicians and patients support the approach of the organization. The next step in early 2010 will be to involve some of China's leading doctors in an expert panel and get their input and support. The resulting guideline will be presented at the World Cardiology Congress in Beijing. Unite for Health has partnered with experts from Shanghai to incorporate an effective approach to lifestyle counseling to prevent heart disease, which it plans to test using a community-based approach. (http://www.uniteforhealth.org)

- **Fitness Forward:** Fitness Forward is a non-profit organization whose mission is to lead children in the United States to live well. The organization envisions a day when all children, regardless of background or circumstance, will grow up with the knowledge, motivation, and tools to live healthier, happier lives. Fitness Forward's signature program, Drive 2 Fitness (D2F), motivates and empowers elementary school children and their families to lead healthier lifestyles through education, web-based tracking tools, social marketing, and incentives. Rishi Shukla, TiE member and Fitness Forward CEO and founding member, said that the TiE-Boston SE Group has helped Fitness Forward identify new business partners, hone its business model, and recruit talented volunteers. Fitness Forward was featured at two of TiE-Boston's most widely attended events, the Global Public Health Conference and the Forum for Social Entrepreneurship (ForSE), both of which were organized by TiE-Boston's SE Group. (http://www.fitnessforward.org)

- **Assured Labor:** Assured Labor creates a digital marketplace for jobs using mobile phones and the Internet. The service is similar to Monster.com, but targets mid-to-low wage workers in emerging markets and leverages mobility to reach workers that are connected by mobile phones but not the Internet. Assured Labor started in 2008 as an entrant in the MIT 100K Business Plan Competition. It had its sights set on bringing transparency to day-labor and low-wage job markets in India, China, Brazil, and Africa. The SE Group worked with Assured Labor to refine their business plan as they prepared to launch their pilot. A panel of senior charter members reviewed early versions of the plan, provided constructive direction, and subsequently helped introduce them to a number of sources for their initial round of funding. In addition, Assured Labor was one of the featured speakers at the widely attended Forum for Social Entrepreneurs in 2008. (http://www.assuredlabor.com)

- **India School Fund:** India School Fund (ISF) was founded a couple of years ago by five MIT and Harvard students, with the goal of ensuring effective delivery of high-quality education to poor villages in India to break the vicious cycle of poverty and to empower the local population. Their first project was the establishment of a school in Rajugella where faculty from the prestigious Rishi Valley Public School was hired to provide high-quality education to over 240 students. ISF wanted to expand its efforts to provide adult literacy and create microbusiness opportunities for people in the village. They presented to TiE-Boston SE Group which was able to connect them with the TARAkshar program provided by Development

Alternatives to bring adult literacy to the village. TIE-Boston SE members also served as mentors for the microbusiness development initiative and helped bring education technology to scale the program. (http://www.indiaschoolfund.org)

- **YEA:** Julie Nessen founded Young Entrepreneurs Alliance (YEA) in 2001 to empower at-risk teens through business ownership. YEA helps low-income teens realize their economic potential and take steps toward financial independence by owning and running viable businesses that operate within their schools. With a successful start, YEA was looking for direction and help in managing its next stage of growth. Its business model was based on direct service with 97 percent of its funds coming from philanthropic sources. It was now looking to diversify and franchise its success to generate an income stream. It was also looking to leverage corporate community involvement and staff development activities. YEA initially presented its work at an SE Group Steering Committee meeting that led to several introductions within the TiE network. Julie was also invited to speak at the ForSE: Forum for Social Entrepreneurs conference. Using a case study exercise YEA was able to tap into the collective experience and inputs of more than 50 professionals drawn from various disciplines to brainstorm a number of alternative solutions. YEA is currently in the process of executing its next phase of growth based on the rich range of options that it captured from the diverse business audience at ForSE. (http://www.yeaworks.org)

These are examples of a few successes that the SE Group has nurtured over the short period of time that it has been in existence. As word of its work has spread, it has also been able to build strong partnerships with other organizations active in this field. We have partnered with international and national groups like Ashoka, Grameen, New Profit, and the Acumen Fund and also with local organizations like Community Consulting Partners and Social Innovation Forum. Together we have helped each other grow and nurture the next generation of social entrepreneurs.

The success of TiE-Boston's SE ecosystem has begun to spread; TiE chapters in Washington, D.C., Pittsburgh, and Colorado have organized panels or presentations on social entrepreneurship and expressed an interest in starting an SE movement. Most recently, in February 2009, the TiE Delhi chapter held an inaugural event for an SIG dedicated to social initiatives.

We urge the readers of this book to learn from the examples of TiE and the other organizations represented in this book to find purpose in affecting social change. Whether it be economic development, health, or education, the global environment will benefit from the efforts of social entrepreneurs such as those writing about their organizations in the following chapters.

Jugnu Jain
Research Fellow and the Disease Area Expert for Multiple Sclerosis, Vertex Pharmaceuticals, Cambridge, Massachusetts

Raj Melville
Consultant—Marketing and Strategy, Boston, Massachusetts

Rakesh Pandey
Independent Consultant, Boston, Massachusetts
Co-chair, Charter Member Committee, TiE-Boston
Co-founder, Social Entrepreneurship Group, TiE

REFERENCE

Bornstein, David. (2007) *How to Change the World: Social Entrepreneurs and the Power of New Ideas*. Oxford, New York: Oxford University Press.

Preface

This book has been inspired by our involvement with The Indus Entrepreneurs (TiE). TiE is a unique organization that is committed to nurturing and fostering the next generation of entrepreneurs with a twist of social responsibility. In this preface we will explain this unique confluence of creating wealth and giving back that is at the core of TiE. Through networking, mentoring, and education, members and charter members of TiE-Boston, one of TiE's largest chapters, have become passionately involved in giving back and doing good in the process.

In association with TiE-Boston, this book is a compilation of academic thought—articles and practical on the ground experiences of TiE members in the area of social entrepreneurship. Contributing to the recent debates of successful/viable business models and the role of government, NGOs, non-profit and for-profit businesses in socially responsible business, we invited contributions from TiE-Boston members that are presented in this edited volume in the form of a case study or case person or academic issue.

FUNDAMENTALS OF THE INCEPTION OF TIE

How it got started: On a lovely California evening in 1992 a few successful entrepreneurs, corporate executives, and senior professionals had gathered in a hotel room to meet and listen to a visiting dignitary from India. The plane was late and then never came.

Having gathered and waiting, this group from the Indus region decided to go ahead and network with those who had assembled in the room anyway. They met people they did not know lived in Silicon Valley, realized they had a lot in common; that many of them were building companies, others were working on an idea, and still others had a lot of resources to offer whether advice or capital. As the group came to close this first get-together it was proposed that these meetings should continue as they offered great networking value that could also lead to other great things. If nothing came from it at least they all had fun!

Following that several key persons worked hard to organize the follow-up meetings to this initial gathering. It took a lot of faxing agendas and RSVPs to make sure that key members of the group stayed and came to the next few meetings. This helped to keep up the enthusiasm and the momentum for developing the cause. A name was developed for the group, "The Indus Entrepreneurs or TiE," and the idea of TiE was born as an organization that would foster and nurture entrepreneurship through mentoring, networking, and education (TiE Inc., 1992–2002).

In a few years the initial group of Silicon Valley entrepreneurs with roots in the Indian subcontinent developed the philosophical framework for the organization and slowly rolled out a vision of a global organization with multiple chapters. With that in mind the Boston chapter was launched in the spring of 1997 with Desh Deshpande leading the effort.

From this simple concept, TiE has evolved into an open, active, and vibrant organization with three objectives:

- to foster entrepreneurship and to nurture entrepreneurs;
- to network and to facilitate networking among members; and
- to help members engage with the community and give back.

Over the years TiE has become the world's largest not-for-profit organization that fosters entrepreneurship, the key driver of economic growth in every region. Building on its global connectivity, TiE has grown in several countries with over 55 chapters across the globe. Its members raised 6 percent of the US venture capital and have created over $250 billion in wealth for its respective communities.

TiE as an organization and its members are dedicated to the virtuous cycle of wealth creation and giving back to the community with a focus on creating and nurturing the next generation of entrepreneurs. To this end, TiE charter members (a unique group of executive volunteers), members, and sponsors, volunteer their time to lead and deliver on all TiE programs.

Vision for TiE: The philosophical framework developed by the initial team created the context for the organization to grow. These guideposts became important principles by which the organization grew while keeping true to its core (TiE Inc., 2005–2006):

- Create an open, inclusive, and transparent organization;
- Provide positive leadership role models by maintaining high ethical standards;
- Emphasize value-creation through informed entrepreneurship;
- Maintain high ethical standards;
- Display rigorous, intellectual, honest behavior;
- Pursue a modern, scientific, and forward-looking approach;
- Remain socially responsible;
- Disdain pettiness, divisiveness, and corruption; and
- Strive to remain an idea- and value-driven organization.

Several key TiE leaders have become role models by living and working by these standards. In this book we are revisiting this core to explore how these basic philosophical principles, with which the organization started, have panned out in the work, success, and giving back to the community by members of TiE-Boston.

TiE-BOSTON: 1997 TO PRESENT

TiE-Boston was the second-largest TiE chapter to be formed in 1997 after Silicon Valle. Its mission is to "Foster, encourage and support entrepreneurship in the New England region." It is a part of this global TiE group that is the largest not-for-profit organization promoting entrepreneurship. TiE-Boston works to accomplish its goals through various programs on education, mentoring, and networking making TiE the world's largest networking organization for innovators from various fields, including business, academia, government, administration, and non-profits.

TiE-Boston has eight vibrant programs that educate, mentor, and inspire entrepreneurs to get started. With this unique mission "to create entrepreneurs" that add value for our society TiE-Boston has been able to create a multi-tiered ecosystem that supports entrepreneurship. This area of work in our society is underserved and TiE continues to make a significant contribution through its programs that are an engine to drive entrepreneurial opportunities and activities for our society.

THE CHARTER MEMBER: A UNIQUE EXECUTIVE VOLUNTEER

TiE's underlying theme is entrepreneurship. It believes that creation of wealth is a noble purpose. It sees entrepreneurs as a source of energy. How does TiE do that? Although most organizations are typically homogenous in nature, TiE is distinctive in the sense that it facilitates an invitation-only group of charter members who receive and contribute to build the organization by providing resources to aspiring entrepreneurs.

Charter members are successful veteran entrepreneurs, corporate executives, and senior professionals who have reached a stage in their professional life when they are ready, willing, and able to contribute to fellow members. Charter membership is by invitation only, and subject to a due process prescribed in the TiE bylaws. Charter members pay significantly higher annual membership fees thus helping to underwrite some of each TiE chapter's operations.

Charter members are "givers and the engines" of TiE. Charter members are selected by their ability to contribute and willingness to give. They also participate in the leadership and management of TiE chapters.

A key strength of TiE is the unsurpassed quality of its charter members. Seekers in any organization come as and when they find value but the value is created mostly by the "givers." This happens in the several hundred forums that TiE programs create to facilitate strong vertical interaction between the two groups and at the same time attract and retain an unparalleled group of charter members on a global basis.

Furthermore, one of the key objectives of the charter members is to inspire budding entrepreneurs and to increase probability and quality of entrepreneurial success and to accelerate their timing. With this effort some TiE members may become truly successful entrepreneurs, but they in turn continue to inspire hundreds of others.

A core strength of TiE is the quality of its charter members who have achieved professional success and have established a stature in the community. They are the unique shareholders of the organization, who join the group with the willingness to give back to the community of entrepreneurs. Charter members are the executive volunteers who contribute their time, effort, energy, and skills to further the development of their chapters and of their fellow members. They contribute more visibly by the successful companies they build thereby creating jobs, wealth, and prosperity for the state.

While charter members enjoy a number of benefits and net-working opportunities among them, by accepting and/or maintaining membership in the corporation, each charter member is an executive volunteer and may devote some reasonable amount of time and effort to further the purposes and goals of the corporation. They willingly invest time, energy, and resources to mentor budding entrepreneurs. They encourage entrepreneurs to have courage, develop skills, cultivate knowledge, and gather wherewithal to increase the odds of success.

To reinforce TiE mission, the charter members' objectives could be stated as:

- inspire and enable charter members to become better leaders and entrepreneurs;

- inspire and enable members to become better leaders and entrepreneurs;
- help strengthen the culture of entrepreneurship in the Indus region;
- develop intellectual content and manage knowledge dissemination to accelerate entrepreneurship process;
- help TiE become integrated in the mainstream organizations in the world; and
- help promote TiE's charter members and members to positions of global leadership.

The charter member's willingness to give has to extend to three constituencies: members (that is, budding entrepreneurs), other charter members, and TiE itself as a non-profit institution primarily fueled by the energies of the charter members. Thus, it is a charter member's individual initiative, drive, persistence, and willingness to volunteer that propel TiE's growth. A strong networking within these charter members is a necessary condition for the TiE mission to be fulfilled.

TiE-BOSTON'S EIGHT VIBRANT PROGRAMS

TiE-Boston runs eight vibrant programs to educate, mentor, network, and inspire entrepreneurs in the community. With a unique mission to create entrepreneurs that add value to our society, TiE-Boston's programs are an engine to drive entrepreneurial opportunities and activities (Figure 1).

Leaders & Legends: A program that features men and women who have demonstrated extraordinary success and created exceptional value for society. In this series we hear their stories, the challenges they faced, the lessons they learnt and the insights they gained.

TiECON East: TiE's flagship event on the east coast is the annual conference TiECON East, where hundreds of entrepreneurs, venture

FIGURE 1   TiE-Boston's Mission and Programs

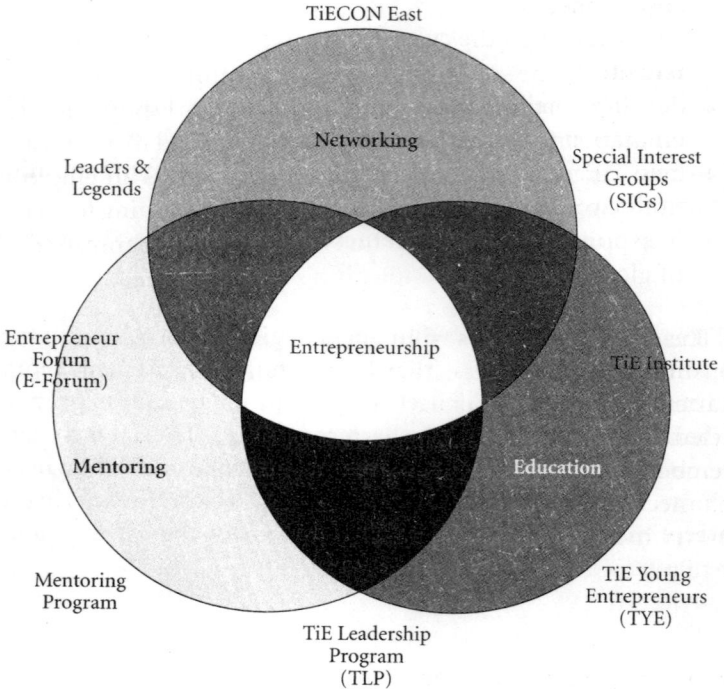

Source: TiE-Boston, 2009 Sponsorship Brochure, Boston, MA.

capitalists, service providers, and would-be entrepreneurs gather together for a program highlighting the latest trends in the world of entrepreneurship. TiECON East is the annual flagship conference organized by TiE-Boston. A consortium of TiE's east coast chapters (including two in Canada) leads TiE-East, and comes together for TiECON East. TiECON attracts important thought leaders, industry stalwarts, and key venture capitalists and is the place to network about your next new opportunity.

Special Interest Groups (SIGs): These are groups that conduct educational sessions on deepening knowledge with a focus on several vertical sectors by addressing cutting-edge issues and opportunities. Ten industry-specific SIGs operate at TiE–Boston from wireless to clean tech to life sciences and many more.

TiE Institute: In the spirit of providing continuing entrepreneurial education TiE Institute provides its members workshops and seminars on acquiring the know-how and skills needed to get ahead in a business career, whether as an entrepreneur or as an employee. TiE Institute programs are organized in a formal learning format on how to sessions, with 101 workshops, lectures, boot camp, or short seminars focused on developing both soft and hard skills.

TiE Leadership Program (TLP): A program developed by the TiE-Boston chapter trains young professionals to become future leaders and entrepreneurs. Participants are encouraged to explore the limits of their leadership capabilities, try out new ideas, develop new skills, and go through a transforming personal development program.

Entrepreneur Forum (E-Forum): This is a platform to facilitate direct interaction between entrepreneurs seeking capital, mentoring, or advice from VCs, Angels, CMs, and other service providers within the TiE ecosystem and is held annually during TiECON East.

TiE Young Entrepreneurs (TYE): Launched by TiE-Boston in 2005, this is a program for high school students (grades 9–12) where volunteers from TiE-Boston teach students what it takes to be an entrepreneur or think entrepreneurially. The program follows a curriculum that covers the study of taking an idea and developing it into a viable and scalable business model and participating in a $10K business plan competition. Students in the program discover the excitement and the reward of participating in the real world of entrepreneurship.

TiE Enter: TiE Enter fosters and supports a culture of entrepreneurship with a primary focus on first-time entrepreneurs, especially undergraduate, graduate students at universities and young professionals. It takes TiE's mentoring programs and small networking sessions of student entrepreneurs on campuses.

In addition to these programs, a highly developed **mentoring program** works across all TiE-Boston's programs, and enables aspiring entrepreneurs to seek, meet, learn from, and receive advice and guidance from more-experienced entrepreneurs in the TiE ecosystem.

Mentoring is an advising relationship that happens one on one between a mentor and mentee for a sustained period of time, typically lasting a year. Mentors have powerful conversations with their mentees which inspire, challenge, teach, and encourage budding entrepreneurs to stay the course.

Mentoring is not just for start-up phase but something entrepreneurs need throughout, at the creativity stage but also at the growth stage or at a time of crisis of leadership. Indeed we need powerful conversations and mentoring throughout our professional careers. Mentoring is a powerful tool that brings value to TiE members.

The Boston chapter has a highly developed mentoring program which takes place within various programs like the SIGs, the TLP, through a more structured online-matching mentoring. A new office-hour mentoring was launched in 2008. More informal mentoring takes place through networks of trust. This is made possible because of the unique shareholder concept of charter members of TiE, who join the group with the understanding that they are willing to give back to the community of entrepreneurs. They provide their time and advice to other entrepreneurs to further build successful companies thereby creating jobs, wealth, and prosperity for the state.

> We became Charter Members to mentor younger Entrepreneurs. We learn one third by reading, one third by doing and the final one third by teaching. The opportunity to mentor is a great way for us not only to help others but to develop further insight into Entrepreneurship. ("Desh" Deshpande, first President and Chairman Emeritus of the Boston chapter, in a personal correspondence)

> Mentoring is the bedrock around which our activities are organized. It is the value differentiator that sets us apart from others. (Apurv Bagri, past Chairman, TiE Global, in a personal correspondence)

Through mentoring TiE sees the possibility of creating a virtuous cycle of entrepreneurship and wealth creation. (Prahalad, 2000)

Vanita Shastri

REFERENCES

Prahalad, C. K. (2000) "The House of TiE," a position paper from TiE-Global, Santa Clara, CA.

TiE Inc. (1992–2002) *Building the Entrepreneurial Ecosystem*, Tenth Anniversary Report, TiE Inc., Santa Clara, CA.

———. (2005–06) *Fostering Entrepreneurship Globally*, Annual Report, TiE Inc., Santa Clara, CA.

Acknowledgements

Both Preeta Banerjee and Vanita Shastri, co-editors of the volume, would like to acknowledge the efforts of certain individuals and organizations that helped put this book together. This book arose from a panel, entitled "From Corporate Social Responsibility to Global Social Entrepreneurship: Achieving Social, Environmental, and Economic Responsibility," on September 18, 2008 at Brandeis University. They thank the Brandeis International Business School that hosted this event that gave rise to this book. A special thanks to Vicky Wu and Christianna Beebe at Executive Minds for Social Innovation (EMSI).

They also thank and deeply appreciate the efforts of all the authors who have worked patiently with deadlines and submitted their chapters to them in time. They thank all TiE members, especially Al Kapoor, President of TiE-Boston, for their support in this endeavor.

Preeta would like to thank her family (Roopom, Probir, Sajal, Archita, Papia, Rishi, and Olympia) for the support and proofreading, especially her newborn Sireeta for letting her work during naptime. Vanita would like to thank and acknowledge her family (Shekhar, Veda, and Kartik) for their support and help toward the completion of this volume. A special thanks to Shekhar Shastri for his inspiration to put out a book like this one acknowledging the work of TiE in the larger community, society, and world.

CHAPTER 1

From Corporate Social Responsibility to Global Social Entrepreneurship

Vanita Shastri and *Preeta M. Banerjee*

Social responsibility has become one of the key business trends of the past decade. Almost every Fortune 100 company now makes meaningful charitable contributions each year. Several have invested significant executive time into innovative corporate/non-profit partnerships. Responsible organizations have now set even more aggressive goals of social, environmental, and economic sustainability.

Corporate social responsibility or CSR as a concept has been constantly evolving from its emergence as method for companies to make charitable donations and show their shareholders their "commitment" to social issues in their societies. The concept today is moving away from a "shareholder alone" focus to a "multi-stakeholder focus." This would include investors, employees, business partners, customers, regulators, local communities, the environment, and society at large.

The triple bottom line approach to CSR emphasizes a company's commitment to operate in an economically, socially, and environmentally sustainable manner. In the current state of globalization it has become important for companies to adopt a CSR strategy as it reflects on the social impact policy of the company. We find that companies that support social responsibility do so, because at the core of the company there is an entrepreneur or change agent who is passionate about looking at the planet holistically.

This book argues that the global village is moving from CSR to the global social entrepreneur (GSE) who is making impact in multiple ways in multiple locations at the same time. The contribution of a globalized world and the exchange of ideas and best practices of the previous era have made the emergence and work of the GSE more feasible. The book outlines a number of significant cases of this new phenomenon as well as the exchange of global practices in the social sector.

THE MULTIPLE FACES OF SOCIAL RESPONSIBILITY

Social responsibility is the combined effort by mankind to make this world a safer, more nurturing, and caring place. Environmental sustainability is a key to protect the planet and keep it safe for several generations. In this book we explore organizations that are doing this through innovative ways globally.

Environmental sustainability is the hope for this planet to maintain the life-reinforcing capabilities so that human life along with all the other species, animal, and minerals can be sustained in the physical environment. So that the natural habitat, that we now take as a given, will survive for the future.

Separating out what processes are good for mankind and the planet in the long run is becoming more complex. Numerous terms and methods emerge each year that obfuscate our understanding. "Biofarming" is one such term that sounds eco-friendly, but is used by biotechnology firms to get federal approval for farming plants that are genetically modified for use in making drugs. Other food companies and environmentalists argue that the genetically altered variety of plants could cross-pollinate with other food crops and thus introduce foreign genes in the regular food chain. A good example was the case of Anheuser Busch (the number one buyer of rice and the largest brewer in the United States) refusing to buy rice from the state of Missouri if genetically modified medical crops were allowed to be grown in the state. These practices increasingly make clear that what we do individually is not enough but what our neighbor does is as important since it is going to impact our life in the long term as well. Hence, local connections have far reaching global interconnections and impact and thus consequences for us all. In a globalized world these interconnections are becoming more intertwined.

A new movement on business transformation called "Conscious Capitalism" is gaining ground in the United States. Several leading academicians and business leaders are at the forefront of this initiative of reinventing "capitalism with a conscience and a sense of interconnectedness." In his book, *Firms of Endearment* (Sisodia et al., 2007), Professor Raj Sisodia argues that several companies are succeeding in the marketplace by striving to get a *share of the heart of the consumer rather than their wallets*. Conscious capitalism is then about a fundamental realignment of the business purpose. John Mackey, CEO, Whole Foods Market is one such leader who writes in his paper, "Conscious Capitalism: Creating a New Paradigm for Business," that the world has become much more complex since … simple machine metaphors were first developed…. We will need to create a new business paradigm that moves beyond simplistic machine/industrial models to those that embrace the complex interdependencies of multiple constituencies. The cases in this book push for this idea that if interest of all stakeholders is pursued toward a higher purpose, eventually everyone gains.

4 ❖ Vanita Shastri and Preeta M. Banerjee

UNDERSTANDING THE SOCIAL ENTREPRENEUR

A social entrepreneur is an actor who seeks to solve or engage with a key social issue. Increasingly actors connecting these two concepts of social responsibility and environmental sustainability fall in the realm of social entrepreneurship.

The Social Entrepreneur

While the business entrepreneur has been studied for a long time the spotlight on the social entrepreneur is more recent. As Bornstein argues in his book, *How to Change the World*, this is because for a long time social entrepreneurs were viewed as "humanitarians or saints" and the stories of their work were narrated more as "stories" than as case studies (Bornstein, 2007). It is only recently that the work of social entrepreneurs has begun to receive the rigorous scrutiny of both academic and field methodology to ascertain best practices and learnings from the cases.

In the social realm ideas are given greater importance. Victor Hugo's famous statement, "There is one thing stronger than all the armies in the world and that is an idea whose time has come," is often cited as the powerful backing for this line of explanation. But in reality there are several ideas over which there may be general consensus in any society or in the world but despite such a consensus we find little real or effective implementation of social programs. Ideas, like access to primary education, or ending poverty and hunger for all are good examples of such ideas.

Nandan Nilekani in his book new book, *Imagining India* (2009), categorizes ideas into four groups:

- Ideas that have arrived: A group of ideas on which there is consensus and good amount of policy implementation.
- Ideas in progress: Issues around which there is broad consensus but much remains to be done for a successful completion of policy implementation.

- Ideas in battle: Those issues that are still being debated and need a consensus.
- Ideas to anticipate: Those issues that are out there, but not being addressed yet.

While he divides issues into these categories for India the schema is interesting for the social sector as a whole and provides an interesting methodology to address issues.

Thus, in the social realm any idea needs its champion—the architect who is so driven and passionate about the cause or idea that they are willing to dedicate a lifetime of work toward its end. Social change results because there are "obsessive people who have the skill, motivation, energy and bullheadedness to do whatever is necessary to move them forward" (Bornstein, 2007: 94) on an idea and implement it as a program.

The Finance Minster of India in 1992, Manmohan Singh (who became the prime minister in 2004 and 2009), at the end of his first budget speech quoted Victor Hugo's foregoing statement as well. However, as I argue in this chapter an idea supported by a key agent or agency is the important glue for its successful implementation. As researching economic policy change illuminated, ideas for change were floating in various ministries and the Prime Minister's Office but it is more than just "ideas whose time has come" that is needed to implement an idea into policy fruition (Shastri, 1995: 248). In the economic realm it is often a crisis of sorts that pushes real meaningful change, as was in the case of India in 1992.

When we examine closer some of the best cases of success in the social sector, we find that at the core of the idea was a passionate person driven by the purpose or cause of concern working with "vision, drive, integrity of purpose and great persuasive powers and remarkable stamina" (Bornstein, 2007: 94).

An entrepreneur is one who looks to find a solution when faced with a problem. Desh Deshpande, an accomplished entrepreneur and philanthropist, describing the three most salient characteristics of an entrepreneur at a TiE event said, "An entrepreneur is one, who when faced with a problem does not complain." An entrepreneur operates in a solution space which means that s/he looks to find ways to solve problems and third, an entrepreneur is one who takes action and is thus a doer. An entrepreneur goes out and tries to solve the problem by working with a better solution. In the world of technology, that could be with better and faster technology but in the social sector this would be individuals with innovative solutions to society's most pressing social problems.

Social entrepreneurship is the work of an individual or a team that recognizes a social problem and uses entrepreneurial principles to organize, create, and manage a venture to make social change. Social entrepreneurship can be found in an ecosystem of established firms, business entrepreneurs, government organizations, and NGOs and non-profit organizations. Social entrepreneurs are often so driven by their idea that they commit their whole lives to changing the direction of their field. They are both visionaries and ultimate realists concerned with the practical implementation of their vision.

As Bill Drayton of Ashoka said, "People understand this field by anecdote rather than theory" (quoted in Bornstein, 2007: 117). He spent some good amount of time on this issue. He interviewed hundreds of social entrepreneurs and from their stories and anecdotes was able to see the patterns that helped him distill the "principles" that he uses to characterize a social entrepreneur. There are several intangibles that work toward the success of the social entrepreneurs, who may not have the writing skills or the level of education of leaders in other sectors but have the passion, vision, determination, and ethics.

Six qualities of a successful social entrepreneur emerged:

- willingness to self correct;
- willingness to share credit;
- willingness to break free of established structures;
- willingness to cross disciplinary boundaries;
- willingness to work quietly; and
- strong ethical impetus.

Emergence of the Global Social Entrepreneur:
Best Practices from Cases in the Book and Beyond

Some of the cases included in the book bring out the unique models of development that have been developed by global social entrepreneurs. The evolution of the social sector has progressed in the direction of learning from best practices. Hence, we find ample scope for transference of knowledge supported by communications technology in today's world. Here are some examples of how the work of these organizations is generating best practices that are being learnt and transferred to other organizations.

The unique method by which Akshaya Patra of India feeds 1 million schoolchildren every day demonstrates how an idea was implemented in a scalable and fool proof way. Today the global foundation for the group, The Akshaya Patra Foundation or TAPF, supported by the Deshpande Foundation is providing lessons to numerous organizations across the globe to transfer, localize, and implement the model elsewhere (Chapter 2).

The key elements of organizing local community for implementing social programs are an important ingredient of the Pratham model. First, Pratham developed a unique pedagogy to teach basic literacy skills for primary education that is scalable. Second, it developed a unique model to recruit and train teachers and community organizers; and third, Pratham paid attention to data collection of all its work in every field from the very beginning. Hence, it became a leader in reporting metrics. These aspects of its work made it a natural partner of the Government of India in assessing the status of education in the country. Some of these "best practices" emerging from Pratham's experience are discussed in Chapter 4.

The Self Employed Women's Association (SEWA) was started by a visionary, Ela Bhatt, who set out to unionize unorganized women workers who had no resources and no rights. It was registered as a trade union in 1972 to bring together women workers to protect their rights and develop resources for their empowerment, finance, insurance, and health. The organization has become such a force that it inspired women in the United States to set up a similar organization called "Women in Informal Economy, Globalizing and Organizing" (www.wiego.org) that is supported by United Nations and the Ford Foundation to work in several countries in Africa and Asia.

Grameen Bank, a key innovator in providing microfinance in Bangladesh has become a leader in setting up and inspiring others in the microfinance sector. The Grameen Bank itself has started branches in the USA and other parts of the world.

ORGANIZATIONS AND THE CONCEPT OF GIVING—THE CASE OF TiE

Tying Social Responsibility to Correct Business Practices

In this section we explain this unique confluence of creating wealth and giving back that is at the core of an organization like The Indus Entrepreneurs or TiE. TiE is an exemplar organization in that, while committed to nurturing and fostering the next generation of entrepreneurs it also has a strong commitment to social responsibility.

In association with TiE-Boston, this book is a compilation of academic thought—articles and practical on-the-ground experiences of TiE members in the area of social entrepreneurship, charitable foundations, clean technology for managers, academics, and government officials.

A number of members and charter members of TiE-Boston, one of TiE's largest chapters, have become passionately involved in giving back to the community and doing good in the process. Contributing to the recent debates of successful/viable business models and the role of government, NGOs, non-profit and for-profit businesses in socially responsible business, we invited contributions from TiE-Boston members that are presented in this edited volume in the form of a case study or case person or academic issue.

Fundamentals of Giving at TiE

In the Preface we described that TiE as an organization emerged with the objective of the development for those in need. (See Preface for more details on the TiE organization.) TiE members began to give back to their fellow members and community from the very start of the organization in 1992. A main thrust of the organization was to engage with the community and contribute to its development.

Over the years TiE has become the world's largest not-for-profit organization that fosters entrepreneurship in every arena including social entrepreneurship. Toward this end, TiE charter members (a unique group of executive volunteers), members, and sponsors volunteer their time to lead and deliver on all TiE programs.

The philosophical framework of the organization had included from the very beginning principles like "remain socially responsible." Several key TiE leaders have become role models by living and working by these standards. In this book, we present this basic philosophical principle with which TiE as an organization was started, and show how it has resulted in contributing to the growth of not just corporate social responsibility but to the emergence of global social entrepreneurship.

A Unique Executive Volunteer: TiE Charter Members

TiE's underlying theme is entrepreneurship. It believes that creation of wealth is a noble purpose but doing good at the same time could be intertwined to this process. It sees entrepreneurs as a source of energy and engines of development and growth. Although most organizations are typically homogenous in nature, TiE is distinctive in the sense that it facilitates an invitation-only group of charter members who contribute to build the organization by providing resources for other aspiring entrepreneurs.

Charter members are "givers and the engines" of TiE. Charter members are selected by their ability to contribute and willingness to give. Thus, it is a charter member's individual initiative, drive, persistence, and willingness to volunteer that propel TiE's growth.

Giving Back

To the local TiE chapter: Charter members of TiE-Boston have created innovative technology solutions for crucial problems and built companies that have done well thereby becoming successful in their own personal lives as well. They have also engaged in innovative ways to give back to the TiE community. By volunteering for TiE programs they mentor, educate, and point resources to other aspiring entrepreneurs. They run various programs of the chapter and are passionate about the work TiE does.

To the community and society: Beyond the local TiE chapter, charter members and members of TiE are engaged with the community both locally in the USA and also connect and contribute to the development of the Indus region as a whole. From building a world-class school in their own village, to starting and running a country-wide engineering competition in India, to establishing a foundation that takes on development work seriously, TiE members have covered it all. In the chapters that follow these member initiatives for social good and sustainability are explored.

One direct example of how philanthropic efforts of TiE members created a new global non-profit group is when the group supported the Silicon Valley United Community Appeal (UCA) fundraiser in California to support the victims of the Gujarat earthquake in 2001. This effort later resulted in the formation of the America India Foundation (AIF), an ambitious endeavor to cultivate diaspora philanthropy and accelerate social development in India. AIF has grown into a vibrant organization with a unique model that funds multi-stakeholders. A number of TiE-Boston members actively participate in this effort which is detailed in Chapter 5, later in this volume.

The connection to social good and nurturing sustainability was most directly reflected in the creation of a special interest group

(SIG) on social entrepreneurship (SE) by the TiE-Boston chapter in 2006. Boston was the first chapter to launch this initiative that provided a platform for social entrepreneurs to meet, exchange ideas, and develop connections in the city and beyond. The Special Interest Group on Social Entrepreneurship was created with a mission to build a "forum for social, business and technical entrepreneurs with a strong interest in social entrepreneurship ... to assist them in translating that interest into substantial social contributions." The group has grown to become a nucleus around which a number of socially responsible change agents congregate. The new phenomena that we explore in this book are the connections that most of these social organizations have with different parts of the world, and in particular with India. (More information on the TiE Social Entrepreneurship SIG is covered in the Foreword of this volume.)

ORGANIZATION OF THE BOOK

This book is organized in three broad themes. The first theme, consisting of Chapter 2 and Chapter 3, defines social responsibility and environmental sustainability and describes performance measures in each of these areas. The second theme (Chapters 4, 5, 6, and 7) offers four in-depth cases of social endeavors within new and existing organizations. The third and final theme (Chapters 8, 9, 10, and 11) offers four in-depth cases tackling issues of environmental sustainability.

In Chapter 2, Gururaj "Desh" Deshpande (one of the founding members and an exemplar of social entrepreneurship), Meenakshi Verma Agrawal, Nishith Acharya, and Naveen Jha write about the Deshpande Foundation and programs that create true social impact. The Deshpande Foundation is a prominent American philanthropy focused on economic development, health, and education in India and the United States. Success at the Deshpande Foundation is found in scalable solutions that impact millions of lives. In Chapter 3, Duncan White writes about Arup and selecting and setting corporate sustainability measurements. Arup is a global firm of designers, engineers, planners, and business consultants with a culture of sustainability. Sustainability systems can be set up and rolled out in major global organizations by setting appropriate key performance indicators (KPIs) by which sustainability can be measured.

Chapters 4, 5, 6, and 7 give us in-depth cases of organizations that were built for social responsibility and affecting change. In Chapter 4, Leona Christy and Vikas Taneja write about Pratham and building partnerships at different levels of government to create impact. Pratham is an organization that works to improve health, livelihood, and education in India, an India-based organization that has helped over 2 million children achieve literacy and basic mathematics skills. Pratham partners with the Government of India to achieve its mission of "every child is in school … and learning well" (Pratham, 2005). In Chapter 5, Behzad J. Larry, Azad Oommen, and Venkatesh "Venky" Raghavendra write about the American India Foundation (AIF) and how social endeavors can cross national boundaries and have significant impact on both sides despite the distance between them. AIF is a non-profit American development organization that is devoted to accelerating social and economic change in India. The AIF chapter in Boston was created in 2001, and over the course of the years has become a strong presence in the community with many of its efforts driven by members of TiE-Boston. In Chapter 6, Vibha Pingle writes about Ubuntu at Work and helping women entrepreneurs in areas of extreme poverty. Ubuntu at Work is an organization that helps women microentrepreneurs to build their own businesses. In Chapter 7, Steven F. Young describes his work at Wainwright Bank and introducing social entrepreneurship to a traditionally profit-centered industry. Wainwright Bank grew from zero to a billion dollars in assets by creating a unique brand that has captured worldwide attention as one of the most socially progressive companies within its industry.

Chapters 8, 9, 10, and 11 focus on issues of environmental sustainability. In Chapter 8, Vithal V. Deshpande describes his work in managing stakeholders through education. Success of the environmental sustainability efforts depends on the complex interaction between the government and the stakeholders, or the industry and its stakeholders. This chapter describes the importance of educating stakeholders in developing strategies of interweaving economic, environmental, and social causes to deliver equity, affordability, profitability, that in turn provide sustainability. In Chapter 9, Daniel Wengrovitz and Preeta M. Banerjee describe the clean technology industry as an exemplar of social entrepreneurship and environmental sustainability. Clean technologies are the devices used to capture and distribute energy with less harmful effects on the environment than traditional techniques. This growing industry is a case study in how innovation can be shaped by stakeholders. In Chapter 10, Ameeta Soni describes her work at VFA and current developments in green building. VFA is the leading provider of integrated software and services for facilities asset management and capital planning across a wide range of industries. In Chapter 11, Sushil Bhatia describes his experience in building new products that not only help the environment but also help the bottom line of the companies. His development of DeCopier paper cleaning products can help social entrepreneurs understand different approaches that companies need to take for developing new green and sustainable products.

REFERENCES

Bornstein, David. (2007) *How to Change the World: Social Entrepreneurs and the Power of New Ideas.* Oxford, New York: Oxford University Press.

Mackey, John. "Conscious Capitalism: Creating a New Paradigm for Business." Available online at http://www.flowidealism.org/2007/Downloads/Conscious-Capitalism_JM.pdf (accessed on 3 May 2010).

Nilekani, Nandan. (2009) *Imagining India: The Idea of a Renewed Nation.* New York: Penguin Press.

Pratham. 2005. "About Us." Available online at http://prathambooks.org/aboutus.htm (accessed on 3 May 2010).

Shastri, Vanita. (1995) "The Political Economy of Policy Formation in India: The Case of Industrial Policy, 1948–94," Unpublished Ph.D. Dissertation, Cornell University.

Sisodia, Raj, Wolfe, David, and Sheth, Jag. (2007) *Firms of Endearment: How World Class Companies Profit from Passion and Purpose*. New Jersey: Wharton School Publishing.

TiE Inc. (1992–2002) *Building the Entrepreneurial Ecosystem*. Tenth Anniversary Report, TiE Inc., Santa Clara, CA.

TiE Inc. (2005–06) *Fostering Entrepreneurship Globally*. Annual Report, TiE Inc., Santa Clara, CA.

CHAPTER 2

Defining Metrics for Social Impact

Gururaj "Desh" Deshpande, Meenakshi Verma Agrawal, Nishith Acharya, and Naveen Jha

In this chapter, we describe the work of the Deshpandes as an exemplar to what it means to be socially responsible and give back to the community, especially in ways that are environmentally sustainable. We then define metrics used to measure social impact in programs initiated by the Deshpandes.

"Innovation leads to social change," said Desh Deshpande at a recent awards ceremony for a business plan competition for social entrepreneurs in India.

Desh and Jaishree Deshpande are the trustees of the Deshpande Foundation (DF), a prominent American philanthropy focused on agriculture, education, livelihood, health, and globalization in India and the United States. The foundation is committed to two regional centers—Boston, MA and Hubli, Karnataka. Gururaj "Desh" Deshpande is co-founder and chairman of Sycamore Networks, Inc. Prior to co-founding Sycamore Networks, Dr Deshpande was founder and chairman of Cascade Communications Corp.

Dr Deshpande serves as a member of the MIT Corporation, and his generous donations have made possible MIT's Deshpande Center for Technological Innovation.

Also, DF believes and supports innovation in development—through this, their vision of the "Sandbox of Global Innovation" was created in the North-West region of Karnataka state, India. This region, which covers a population of about 10 million people in five districts, has been coined "the Sandbox." The development of Sandbox provides for unique opportunities in social innovation for entrepreneurs, NGO professionals, and students. Working with more than 65 NGO partners in the region, the DF team works function with three main principles:

- **Innovative ideas**—simple but powerful in its potential and can impact the grassroots work of an organization.
- **Entrepreneurs**—individuals who are passionate about their ideas and go through the challenges of getting it implemented.
- **Scalable solutions**—taking the ideas of entrepreneurs, replicating solutions, and impacting millions of lives.

MIT DESHPANDE CENTER FOR TECHNOLOGICAL INNOVATION

The Deshpande Center was established at the MIT School of Engineering in 2002 to increase the impact of MIT technologies in the marketplace. Founded with an initial donation by Jaishree and Desh Deshpande, the center depends on the financial and professional support of successful alumni, entrepreneurs, and investors to provide a sustainable source of funding for innovative research and guidance to help it reach the marketplace. By funding novel, early-stage research and connecting MIT's innovators to the business community, the center helps promising technologies to emerge.

Since September 2002, the Deshpande Center has:

- reviewed 365 proposals from 192 faculties requesting $42.6 million in funding;

- funded 64 projects with over $7 million in grants;
- supported 52 faculties and their students from a diverse array of departments;
- seen the creation of 10 companies (1 license), capitalized at $88.7 million with 132 employees; and
- engaged 100+ volunteers from the venture and entrepreneur community.

Examples of the innovative research that is supported by the Deshpande Center at MIT include:

- **Information technology (IT):** Researchers have been focusing on a next-generation data transformation tool to facilitate the extraction and transformation of data into one common format that could simplify this complex and expensive process.
- **Biotechnology:** In biotech, innovative researchers have created a low-cost, compact, disposable, programmable delivery device using advanced materials technology that could assist individuals with chronic diseases.
- **Nanotechnology:** An example of an interesting project is a method for creating efficient long-lasting portable power sources that could change the battery market.
- **Environmental/development innovations:** To impact development, researchers have created the phase-change incubator, a revolutionary new incubation technology that enables incubation without electricity and the need for skilled maintenance. Moreover, existing prototypes cost only $100—significantly less than comparable products—which may allow new markets that currently cannot afford incubators to open up.

VENTURE PHILANTHROPY

The Deshpande's family philanthropy has helped provide venture seed funding to help foster the growth of three organizations that are making a significant impact on the development of India. These organizations demonstrated enormous potential both in terms of impact and growth and were awarded venture funding to scale to the next level. The organizations are: The Akshaya Patra Foundation (TAPF), the Public Health Foundation of India (PHFI), and the United Way of India.

TAPF is a unique initiative based in India that strives to provide mid-day meals to underprivileged children in the hope of improving the educational opportunities for the participants. TAPF's mission is that "no child should be deprived of an education because of hunger." These mid-day meals are cooked fresh daily in TAPF's kitchens using local ingredients and local foods. They are feeding over 1,000,000 children per day all over India. For TAPF, the Deshpandes provided funding to build a kitchen in the Sandbox (described in more detail in the following section) and established US headquarters to promote global fundraising. Making an impact on global health was important to the Deshpandes, so they provided venture funding to the PHFI to set up five Indian Institutes of Public Health and assist in the formation of global health partnerships. Finally, the foundation supports the United Way of India creating a culture of civic leadership and a destination for global donations.

THE SANDBOX

The five districts of North-West Karnataka—Dharwad, Haveri, Belgaum, Gadag, and Uttar Kannada—serve as the "Sandbox for Global Innovation" for DF. Based in the city of Hubli, DF has taken a novel approach toward working with the NGO sector. Hubli is among 13 other second-tier cities in India that is slated for enormous growth in the next 10–15 years. The critical issue is overcrowding and urban sprawl at the major metropolitan cities around India (Delhi, Mumbai, Calcutta, Chennai, Bangalore). As these major cities are disproportionately bearing the burden of the globalization of India, the development of the second-tier cities is critical to the next stage of the country's development. Hubli is a city of about 1 million people, has an airport, major universities, and several industries. It is based off NH-4 and close to both Mumbai and Bangalore. Proximity to the financial and technical capitals of India makes Hubli a unique location to centralize the work of DF. The main objective is to create the "Hub" for social entrepreneurship in India, specifically in the Sandbox. The four focus areas of DF are agriculture, education, livelihoods, and health.

Agriculture

The five districts cover about 10 million people, approximately. The Sandbox region is unique because across the five districts, there are three ecological zones. These zones provide for irrigation, dry, and rain-fed farming. Agriculture serves as the primary source of income for over 60 percent of the population. There is a mutual relationship of agriculture and livestock. Key challenges in the region include: increased production costs, excessive use of pesticide, decreasing plot size, destabilized food-crop yields, overexploitation of underground water, land pressure from neighboring city, and water harvesting challenges.

Education

The Indian educational system in the Sandbox region remains extremely competitive yet weak in infrastructure. Policy-wise, public education is supposed to be free and compulsory until the eighth standard. The central government's Integrated Child Development Scheme targets early education years and mid-day meals are required to be provided as a part of a 2001 Supreme Court decision. Government schools are mostly found in rural or suburban areas whereas private schools dominate the market in urban areas. The literacy rate is approximately 70 percent while school attendance is approximately 80 percent, both relatively high compared with other states in India. However, infrastructure at public schools remains weak, little or no access to bathrooms, shortage of drinking water, overcrowding, and lack of good teachers. Challenges include dropout rates of 10 percent by fifth standard and 45 percent by eighth standard. Quality issues include lack of non-traditional learning methods and "rote" learning, inability to recognize or address learning disabilities, poorly trained teachers, and class size. There is a significant gap in terms of who can access education and who cannot between groups such as females, scheduled castes, tribal people, and religious minorities.

Livelihoods and Microfinance

The livelihood sector (and non-agricultural employment, in general) is a major part of the secondary and tertiary sectors of employment. This includes microcredit and microsavings programs and constitutes a major part of the innovation happening in the Sandbox. The rate of female participation is 32.1 percent and the Sandbox contribution to net state domestic product is 15.6 percent. The average growth rate in GDP per worker is 4.9 percent and technology innovations support a lot of the livelihood initiatives in the area (use of smart card and cell phone technology). Key challenges include lack of skills that can support the livelihood beyond sustenance, issues with migration, gender empowerment, scheduled castes/tribes, technology, and keeping up with the latest developments in microcredit and microsavings.

Health

In North-West Karnataka, there is a wide range of government-run hospitals and clinics. The National Rural Health Mission currently supports Village Health Workers in the state. The specific areas of need are HIV/AIDS, antenatal care, and child nutrition. Private practitioners are abundant in the area and provide care to those who can afford it. The life expectancy is an average of 62 years, while the infant mortality rate (IMR) and maternal mortality rate (MMR) are 52 and 195, respectively. Vaccinations are between 60 and 80 percent, and contraception is around 60 percent. Major health issues are malnutrition and anemia, lung infections, disability, and gastro-intestinal problems. Additionally, cancer, diabetes, and heart disease are on the rise. HIV/AIDS rates are disputed, tuberculosis is also common but the actual numbers are not known.

DESHPANDE CENTER FOR SOCIAL ENTREPRENEURSHIP (DCSE)

DCSE was inaugurated in February 2009 by the Honorable Abdul P. Kalaam, former President of India, to develop talent and leadership for the non-profit sector. DCSE includes the following programs:

- Deshpande Fellows Program (DFP): In June 2008, DCSE launched an ambitious program focused on propagating social entrepreneurship. DFP is an opportunity for young social leaders to be trained in the knowledge, skills, and practices necessary for success in the development sector. There are two cohorts every year that produce 25 NGO leaders from each batch.
- Entrepreneur in Residence (SEIR): This initiative seeks to serve as a concentrated hub of activity for budding entrepreneurs to create scalable solutions for social problems. DCSE will function as an incubator for the entrepreneurs and will provide the entrepreneurs with logistical support and access to the center's networks and resources, even during the entrepreneur's exploratory stages.
- Leadership in Development (LEAD): The DCSE is dedicated to fostering strong leadership skills in all LEADers and as such

will provide a compulsory orientation for selected candidates. The orientation will cover marketing and recruitment strategies, motivation, and small group theories, management techniques and more.

- Development Dialogue Conference: The Development Dialogue Conference happens annually in Hubli, Karnatka. Along with DF's partner NGOs, national and international stakeholders attend the conference to discuss the latest trends in NGOs and share best practices.
- NGO Executive Education: The Executive Education program has been created to provide first- and second-tier managers at NGOs with the skills they need to become more successful and efficient.

GLOBAL EXCHANGE PROGRAM

The Global Exchange Program (GEP) was launched by DF in 2008 to leverage existing skills all around the work with the need for expertise in the Sandbox. Through several unique initiatives, the GEP has brought a global perspective to the Sandbox. The three initiatives are:

- **Sandbox Fellowship (SF):** SF is a one-year fellowship for professionals with a Masters, 3–5 years of experience, and a passion for making a strong impact at an NGO. Fellows are placed with one NGO for 1 year and they provide technical, administrative, and resource support to some the DF's strongest NGOs. The Fellows are given a stipend, health insurance, and other resources and are expected to help scale up an organization's programs to get it to the next part of its development. Each Fellow is committed to the mission and vision of the organization and provides the organization with the resources in health, agriculture, livelihood, and education through curriculum design, monitoring and evaluation, fundraising, marketing, surveys, and more. The SF provides the NGOs and Fellows with the support to make this relationship successful. The SF is extremely competitive and aims to become one of the premier fellowships in the development sector.

- **Innovators:** All across the world, college campuses are the centers of innovation for solutions to some of the developing world's most intractable problems. DF works to connect these innovations with the grassroots organizations that have the expertise to give the experiment a quality test-run in addition to on-the-ground advice. During the summer of 2009, DF invited teams from UC-Berkeley and USC-Davis to come and try their experiments in partnership with local NGO partners. Testing out water filters, hand washing systems, educational games to discourage tobacco use, and creating global microclinics are just a few examples of the kind of experimentation that went on during this time. Some of the students were encouraged and others challenged with finding new solutions to address some of the challenges faced by the NGOs. Every summer, DF invites proposals from motivated students from the fields of health, agriculture, livelihood, and education to come and work with local NGO partners to make an impact through an innovation.

- **Impact Fellows:** The Impact Fellows are typically professionals with 5–10 years of expertise in their respective fields that are willing to make a short-term impact in the Sandbox. They provide Executive Education sessions and create programs for the young DFPs to learn more about the sectors. As the Global Exchange Program develops, the Impact Fellows will become a more active component of the Sandbox development initiative.

DEFINING METRICS

The Sandbox for Innovation serves as an experimental playground for those who are excited by innovation in development. By choosing to work in a defined geographic space, the measurement of success can be simplified into best practices or models that can be applied anywhere in India or all over the world. For example, the Agastya International Foundation inspires children to think about their science lessons differently. From a young age, at government schools in Karnataka, children are taught science through theory and equations. According to Agastya, this takes the real learning away from the students and puts it in the hands of the teachers. Agastya builds science models to help creatively teach the fundamentals of science. Instead of reading about the human body, they will look at models that define each vein and artery. Through light bulbs, balls, and wire the children will see the universe around them. Physics becomes experiments with balls, ramps, and Bunsen burners. This is an innovation in the Sandbox because traditional methods of education only encourage memorization and traditional rote learning. This not only can create an aversion to science but it also suppresses the very creative aspects of science that make it exciting. Agastya supports science fair competitions for thousands of children at a time and its program in the Sandbox is affecting at least 1 million students and teachers all over India. This innovation, of making science accessible to all, not only those that perform well in exams can make a significant contribution to the development of science in India as a country. As students become more creative and analytical, they will move beyond the paper and into the future business, laboratories, universities, and classrooms of India. They will indirectly and directly impact the growth of a country in a very impactful way.

Once an organization like Agastya can test out its programs in the Sandbox (whether it is new initiatives or improving old ones) a replicable model will be created to disseminate all over India. DF will also help bring in other funders at this point to promote a culture of multiple support networks for the NGOs. Should these other funders decide to move forward, Agastya can open its science centers all over government schools in India, thus leading the program to scale. Instead of reaching 1 million children and teachers, they will be reaching 10 million, then 100 million, etc. As the organization scales, DF will take more of a supportive role to help Agastya gain access to funding and networks and then DF will move on to the next innovation in health, agriculture, livelihood, and education.

PARTNERSHIPS

As an organization that supports partnerships between its NGOs, DF also collaborates with other organizations to help build the capacity of the NGO network. Two examples of this are Infosys Technologies and Google India. Each relationship, in its distinct way, will impact the work in the Sandbox. Infosys Technologies works with DF to provide 1 year of staff expertise to NGOs in the Sandbox. Infosys pays its staff 50 percent of salary and a guarantee of their position when they return if they choose to take 1 year off to work with NGOs working with DF. Not only has Infosys fostered corporate philanthropy throughout its existence, it is clearly a trailblazer when it comes to setting standards for workplace flexibility in charitable donation of services.

Google India is currently working on making its technology more accessible to the NGOs working in the Sandbox. Through DF's technology initiatives in Executive Education, partner NGOs are becoming more trained in the use of the Internet to increase their capacity and funding. As part of the collaboration with Google India, DF's partner NGOs will be trained in the entire Google Free Application Kit (including spreadsheets, documents) in order to increase the efficiency at the NGO and provide it with the core competency to use technology as a sophisticated resource to address growth challenges.

As DF continues to grow and thrive, it will expand in many ways. Staff expansion will certainly be a part of that, as the projects, innovations, and ideas do keep the current staff of 20 (16 in India and four in the United States) very engaged and occupied. DF will also register as a charity in India (80-G) in addition to being a 501c3 organization in the United States. This will help bring more national recognition to the work being conducted in the Sandbox. The organizational environment has the look and feel of a start-up (young and vested professionals working together) while maintaining the professionalism of a corporation.

PLATINUM PARTNER PROGRAM

In Fall 2008, DF launched the Platinum Partner Program, meant to focus on strategic capacity building of two strong partner organizations (Agastya International Foundation and Vidya Poshak). This would include strategic planning with professionals from the fields of business, non-profit management, and corporations. The Deshpandes have also taken a leadership role in these organizations to help them achieve the next level of international recognition and success. An example of how DF has leveraged its networks to successfully support the work of an impactful organization is The Akshaya Patra Foundation (TAPF).

Founded by ISKCON, TAPF provides mid-day meals to over 1,000,000 children all over India daily. When DF began investing in TAPF, the focus was capacity building and strategic planning. DF provided seed money to TAPF to support full-time staff members in the United States, focused primarily on fundraising and awareness building. An ideal Platinum Partner becomes independent of DF's support, sustaining itself through the capacity-building programs that prepare it for a successful future.

CONCLUSION

In conclusion, innovation in the social sector does not happen by accident. It takes a carefully targeted approach that considers both geography and the needs of the population. However, once that target area and community needs are defined, a culture of innovation can be created. Within that culture of innovation, there needs to be a social marketplace for ideas and support, both fiscal and intellectual. Through the Deshpande Center at MIT, venture philanthropy, and the work of DF, something unique has been created. Focused best practices strategies, replicable models, and sustainable programs are the new innovations within the development sector, not just in the Sandbox, but all over the world. We encourage using similar processes for defining social metrics and measuring social impact as illustrated by the programs initiated by the Deshpandes.

CHAPTER 3

Selecting and Setting Corporate Sustainability Measurements

Duncan White

OVERALL OBJECTIVES OF CHAPTER

- To describe the methods by which corporate sustainability systems can be set up and rolled out in a major global organization.
- To discuss the setting of appropriate key performance indicators (KPIs) by which sustainability can be measured.
- To discuss the approach to public reporting (e.g., GRI).

INTRODUCTION

Arup is a global firm of designers, engineers, planners, and business consultants providing a diverse range of professional services to clients around the world. Arup exerts a significant influence on the built environment and is the creative force behind many of the world's most innovative and sustainable designs.

A commitment to the environment and the communities Arup works in has always been at the heart of the company's ethos. This ethos is summarized in the aims of the firm, set out by founder Sir Ove Arup—who believed in integrating environmentalism and social purpose into the firm's work—in his "Key Speech" of 1970.

Although strongly committed to sustainable development and to an active community program for many years, the company had not "articulated" or reported on its activities in these areas until 2007. The company recognized that non-compliance and failure to engage with the environmental, social, and economic issues of the sustainable development agenda could leave it exposed to an increasing variety of non-financial risks. Also, external influences, government policy driven recently by climate change debate, and shifts in public opinion have pushed sustainability to the fore of business operations and reporting for responsible global organizations.

As a result, Arup developed a Sustainability Policy in 2007. Key performance indicators (KPIs) for reporting were subsequently developed, and the first corporate Sustainability Statement was published in 2008. The challenges of implementing a sustainability policy include defining sufficiently tough objectives so as to engender true sustainability benefits to the organization and its clients, and being able to engage and motivate staff in all parts of the world.

The chapter will discuss Arup's approach to formalizing its sustainability policy. It will discuss development and implementation, the identification of sustainability KPIs, the roll-out process, and the approach to public reporting.

MANAGEMENT APPROACH TO SELECTING SUSTAINABILITY MEASURES

The approach to developing Arup's sustainability policy followed the methodology set out here:

- Recognition by the Arup Group Board of the need to implement a formal policy.
- Creation of a formal working group, with representatives from all regions.
- Appointment of a Group Sustainability Director to develop and implement the policy.
- Development of a policy and global KPIs.
- Approval of the policy and KPIs for adoption by the firm.
- The internal implementation of the policy and development of the KPIs.
- The external reporting of the sustainability measures.

KEY CHARACTERISTICS OF THE RIGHT SUSTAINABILITY TEAM

Arup is a global company operating in more than 90 offices in 37 countries. In order to develop and implement a successful sustainability initiative, the team selected to do so needed to not only have the right sustainability qualifications, but the ability to represent and lead the regional/local organizations to implement the business changes the global policy brings.

Arup's Corporate Sustainability team was selected from across the firm. The team is led by a Group Board Director with the ability to drive change from the top of the organization. The rest of the team comprises staff from each of Arup's regions; those who had been most active in developing local sustainability policies and leading projects with a sustainability focus were the natural choices.

BUILDING ON COMPANY CULTURE, HISTORY, AND EXTERNAL INFLUENCES

The company's focus and drive was set by its founder Sir Ove Arup and continues to be strong. Out of his "Key Speech" came 13 original principles which represent the overall aims of the firm, the means by which to achieve them, and the results of this approach. Many of these principles have influenced the formal Sustainability Policy Arup has adopted today.

Arup is at the forefront of thinking about how to create a resilient and sustainable society; one that is socially, environmentally, economically, and culturally sustainable. Arup's approach helps the company not only to answer the questions its clients pose about their current projects, but it provides the ability of the company to add value by helping them to ask different questions and consider the bigger sustainability picture.

An example of this is the Arup sustainability measurement tool, SPeAR™ (Sustainable Project Appraisal Routine), which was developed in 2000 to revolutionize the way companies assess sustainability.

Arup has always been a collaborative organization. Whether the firm is donating its expertise, its time, or its funds (including those donations made through its Charitable Trust), it does do so in a spirit of true partnership. It aims to help other organizations to build their capacity so they can, in turn, make a bigger impact on society. This applies to Arup's humanitarian efforts in the developing world. Endeavors like the Arup Cause—a global initiative, developed in Arup's 60th anniversary year, which aims to encourage and leverage individual capabilities of staff to reduce suffering and improve lives—create structured opportunities for staff to become involved in humanitarian development. In so doing, it celebrates the firm's determination to effect positive change in the developing world, particularly where a lack of access to safe water and sanitation or shelter perpetuates poverty. Arup's Poverty Action Network—a grassroots, umbrella network for staff interested in poverty alleviation, international development, and disaster relief work—continues to grow.

Arup leverages individual and firm-wide capabilities equally in the developed world to give back to society in a meaningful way. Significant investment in research and the company's existing technical, design, creative, and management skills help society understand and deal with the challenges that the future presents. Partnering with key organizations like the Climate Group, the UK Green Building Council, and Hong Kong's Climate Change Business Forum can help those organizations to empower people to change the way they live to improve the built environment and beyond.

The company aims, its history, its recent directions in charitable partnerships and sustainable developments were all strong influencers in setting the direction of the formal corporate sustainability policy.

DEVELOPMENT OF A SUSTAINABILITY FRAMEWORK

A sustainability framework was needed to organize the focus areas and communicate the intent of the program internally and externally. The process for developing the framework consisted primarily of setting up a series of in-person workshops of the core team. These workshops reviewed current company progress in the field of sustainability and considered external drivers.

The external drivers include global environmental aims (e.g., reductions in carbon emissions), recognized global needs (e.g., the needs for the supply of water, sanitation, education, communication to billions of people globally), public/media perception, and the need for financial stability for ongoing operations.

Prior to developing metrics, a framework was developed. This involved benchmarking and reviewing existing frameworks for corporate social responsibility, including:

- Prince of Wales Business and the Environment Guidance for Professional Service Firms;
- Business in the Community (BITC) Framework;
- Triple Bottom Line Approaches (Environmental, Social, Economic or Environmental, Social, Governance);
- Global Reporting Initiative Principles and Guidance;

- Operational Frameworks (Based on Organizational Structure); and
- Frameworks Used by Other Professional Service and Engineering Firms for Reporting on their Performance.

It was determined that the most significant way in which Arup could impact global sustainability challenges was by focusing on its core business—that is, working with its clients to improve the sustainability of their operations, and incorporating a sustainable approach into all projects.

The framework ultimately arrived at consists of four focus areas:

- Our business: Addresses the integration of sustainability into all services and offerings, including training and skills development.
- Our people: Includes social equity, diversity, and caring for Arup's staff.
- Our facilities: Attends to incorporating sustainability into the design and operation of Arup's offices worldwide, including managing its carbon footprint.
- Our external relationships: Addresses the company's relationships with like-minded institutions and charitable partners including monetary donations and staff time commitments.

Once the framework was established, the corporate sustainability team developed a policy which would articulate the firm's commitment and intentions across the four areas. A draft policy was authored and vetted with senior management of the firm in a series of meetings and surveys. The final policy represented the culmination of an intense period of raising awareness and consensus building for integrating sustainability within the firm. It also represented the beginning of a journey to continually improve sustainability performance for the company and its clients.

IDENTIFICATION OF SUSTAINABILITY MEASURES

What gets measured gets managed, and therefore establishing KPIs was an essential step. The team set out to identify measures fitting with the overall objectives of the policy, measures which have a real sustainability impact and which can be calculated by simple but effective metrics.

A materiality test was applied to determine if the indicators represented things that could be measured, or things that really mattered in terms of improving sustainability performance.

The measures chosen were identified to:

- Be relevant to the global Arup business internally and externally;
- Impact areas of economic performance, social impact, and environmental stewardship; and
- Roll up from regional performance into a global sustainability profile.

A list of 13 appropriate, challenging, and measurable global KPIs were selected. Some of these were metrics that had been previously measured as part of the company's internal sustainability activities or normal business operations, and five were new and were set to direct the next generation of the organization.

The company's sustainability KPIs formally reported in 2008 are as follows (Table 3.1):

REPORTING AND ROLL-OUT

In 2007, a sustainability statement was issued. This encompassed the agreed external sustainability measures, but due to the size of the organization and the number of stakeholders, it was considered appropriate for an internal release and review period prior to formal external reporting.

TABLE 3.1 Arup Corporate Sustainability KPI's 2008

Sustainability Policy Objectives	Key Performance Indicators
Our business	**Projects setting sustainability objectives (%)**
• Provide value to clients by building upon its reputation for integrated design and a holistic approach to projects.	Profit (% on turnover)
• Deliver projects recognized for their sustainability credentials, in line with client expectations.	Investments (% of income)
• Evaluate projects with respect to their sustainability risks and opportunities and, where appropriate, discuss these with the client.	Cash at bank (weeks of costs, before profit share)
• Achieve performance that ensures the firm's economic, environmental, and financial viability.	Repeat clients (%)
Our people	
• Employ and retain staff who have a high degree of awareness and expertise in sustainability for all disciplines practised.	Women in the firm (%)
• Provide continual education and training for all staff on sustainability issues relevant to the firm's businesses.	Women in management positions (%)
• Support innovative approaches to implementation of sustainability strategies on projects.	Staff sustainability training (%)

Our facilities

• Maintain management systems to assist with implementation of sustainability objectives.	Staff in offices with EMS to ISO14001 (%)
• Aim to use resources efficiently and to minimize waste, usage of water, energy, and their consumables in the office environment.	Carbon emissions per employee
• Develop a strategy to move toward minimizing carbon emissions in its operations.	Total wastes per employee
• Endeavor to prevent pollution within the scope of its activities.	Lost time accidents
• Develop a strategy for the firm to move toward sustainable procurement of the goods and services used in its operations.	

Our external relationships

• Partner with organizations that practise sustainability and that enable the exchange of ideas and the promotion of sustainability leadership across its businesses.	Charitable donations (£, to nearest £000)
• Fund and work on community projects that achieve sustainability goals.	Pro-bono engagement (£ equivalent staff cost, to nearest £000)

Source: Arup.

During this internal release period, feedback was received from relevant business and staff leaders which enabled the formal external report to be released with appropriate buy-in and updates.

In 2008, Arup released its first corporate sustainability report as part of the annual corporate report for the year ending March 2008. This is intended to be released on an annual basis in the future.

The sustainability goals are now being introduced to everyday business activities. This includes reviewing, reporting, and providing guidance to the business at regional and office management levels. The policy is proving a key document for driving focused sustainable improvements to the company's operations, to its clients, and to the consulting projects being undertaken by the company.

Arup considered Global Reporting Initiative (GRI) principles and indicators in development of its corporate sustainability program, engagement with its key stakeholders (staff and clients), and reporting process. The company has been a key partner in developing GRI's G3 Corporate Sustainability Guidelines used by over a thousand corporations globally. GRI G3 currently has very few indicators relevant to professional service firms like Arup; however, the company is working with GRI to develop a sector supplement for professional services organizations for future implementation and public reporting.

CLOSING DETAIL

Public and corporate interest in sustainability has increased in the 5 years prior to 2009 to the degree that any credible public or private organization needs to consider its approach to sustainability and its public reporting of it. Implementing policies and measurement tools that enhance existing operations and that develop public and/ or business credibility can bring significant internal and external benefits. Selecting appropriate measures, reporting approaches, internally and externally, selecting an appropriate development and roll-out team, and top-level executive commitment and direction of the process are all essential parts of the implementation of a successful sustainability policy.

C H A P T E R   4

Lessons from Working with the Government of India: The Story of Pratham

Leona Christy and *Vikas Taneja*

One in every two children in India—approximately 100 million—cannot read fluently or do simple arithmetic (ASER Centre, 2010). A problem of this magnitude requires a rapid and large-scale intervention. At the same time, the impact of the intervention needs to be sustained over time.

For a non-profit organization that is interested in bringing about large-scale change on a rapid and yet sustained basis, working with the government offers several advantages. However, it also brings with it several challenges, especially in a large and diverse country like India. The education scenario in India varies widely from state to state: while some like Kerala have near universal literacy, others like Bihar and Rajasthan are still trying to ensure that all children are enrolled in schools. Government priorities in the area of education thus tend to be different in each state. Moreover, in a developing country, multiple demands exist for scarce government resources. A non-profit organization that seeks to work with the government needs to be aware of these constraints.

Pratham, India's leading non-profit organization, has evolved a unique relationship with the government at the national, state, and local levels, which promises to teach basic literacy and numeracy skills to over 60 million children of ages 6–14 years all across India. At the same time, Pratham is also acting as a catalyst to improve the efficiency and effectiveness of the immense government investment in primary education.

This chapter lays out the primary education context in India and the work of Pratham. It identifies some of the advantages of working with the government and presents possible entry points and structures for organizations interested in developing similar relationships. Finally, it identifies some of the challenges of working with the government and outlines options in cases where a partnership does not emerge.

THE INDIAN EDUCATION CONTEXT

The Indian national and state governments together spend over $18 billion every year on primary education. In 2001–02, the governments jointly launched Sarva Shiksha Abhiyaan (SSA) or "Education for All" in order to ensure universal primary education for all children of ages 6–14 years.

Although the focus of SSA was initially on improving basic school infrastructure, including school construction, teacher recruitment, and mid-day meals, in recent years the issue of improving education quality has received increasing prominence. The objectives of SSA include the following (DoSEL, 2010):

- All children in school, Education Guarantee Centre, Alternate School, "Back-to-School" camp by 2003.
- All children complete 5 years of primary schooling by 2007.
- All children complete 8 years of elementary schooling by 2010.

- Focus on elementary education of satisfactory quality with emphasis on education for life.
- Bridge all gender and social category gaps at primary stage by 2007 and at elementary education level by 2010.
- Universal retention by 2010.

ABOUT PRATHAM, ASER, AND READ INDIA

Pratham (meaning "first" or "primary") is India's leading non-profit organization in the area of primary education. Its mission is to ensure that every child is in school and learning well. Pratham's focus is thus on ensuring access to quality education for all.

Pratham was founded in 1994 in the slums of Mumbai by Dr Madhav Chavan and Farida Lambay. The initial seed money was provided by UNICEF and the Mumbai Municipal Corporation, which were looking to support a social initiative to ensure universal primary education in Mumbai. Today, Pratham is implementing programs in rural and urban areas in 21 states across India.

In 2000, Pratham was one of three innovative organizations shortlisted for the World Bank's Global Development Network award. Pratham's programs are unique because they are low cost and scalable. Pratham also believes in improving the efficiency of current systems rather than building parallel ones.

Since 2005, Pratham has facilitated the Annual Status of Education Report (ASER), a nationwide survey of children's basic learning levels in India. All rural districts are covered by the survey. Local groups conduct ASER by testing the reading and arithmetic skills of over 700,000 children every year. They also disseminate the findings and look for ways to improve the educational situation in the district. ASER, which is released every year by the Deputy Chairperson of the Planning Commission, has emerged as a major advocacy tool and a credible source of information used by government agencies to design, plan, and implement programs more effectively.

In 2005, ASER, a Pratham-facilitated nationwide survey of children's learning levels, found that although more than 94 percent of children in the age group 6–14 years were enrolled in school, less than half knew how to read or do simple arithmetic problems even by grade 5. Recognizing that rapid, large-scale action was required to address the problem of poor learning in schools, Pratham launched its flagship program, Read India, in April 2007. Read India aims to improve the basic literacy and numeracy skills of children in India of ages 6–14 years and to catalyze government resources to ensure that these improvements are sustained.

The accelerated learning techniques perfected by Pratham over the last few years form a key element of Read India. These techniques have been tested in multiple rural and urban settings and are proven to teach a child to read in less than 2 months. Pilot projects conducted in the states of Maharashtra and Madhya Pradesh confirmed that these results are replicable on a large scale.

Read India has four key elements:

- Time: Focused time spent daily, either in schools or in communities, on activities that build the reading and arithmetic skills of children.
- People: Working with schoolteachers and community volunteers to equip them to work with children.
- Materials: Generating and distributing age-appropriate graded reading materials on scale.
- Monitoring and evaluation: Both internally and through external agencies.

Read India has achieved impressive milestones in its very first year. It has reached over 21 million children in over 358,000 villages across 19 states. Over 800,000 teachers and 375,000 volunteers have been trained. One of the critical factors behind the rapid scaling up of Read India has been the partnerships that Pratham has established with 15 state governments. The impact of Read India has also been greatest in states like Chhattisgarh and Himachal Pradesh where a strong partnership exists with the state government. Figure 4.1 shows the impact of the Read India on reading fluency among

FIGURE 4.1   Percentage of Children Who Can Read Fluently, by Grade

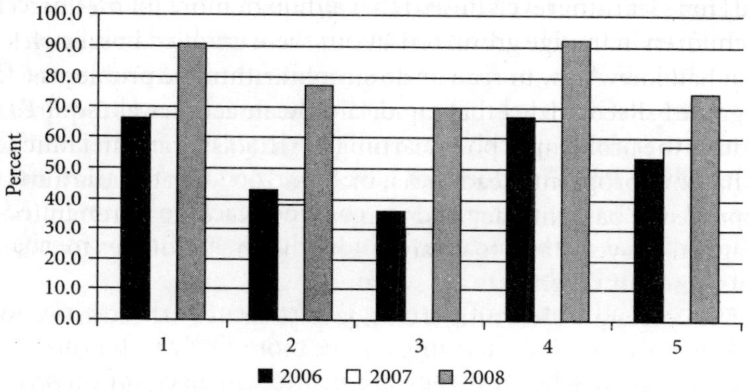

Source: AIF, created for this chapter.

children who study in grades 1 to 5. There was no change between 2006 and 2007. However, Read India, which was implemented jointly by Pratham and the state government in 2007–08, has resulted in large improvements across grades.

RATIONALE FOR WORKING WITH THE GOVERNMENT

Although one can argue that government partnerships are not necessary to Read India or to any other program that aims to bring about social impact on a large scale, having one in place undoubtedly brings with it several advantages, especially in India. Since almost all children in India are enrolled in school and the vast majority of these are studying in government schools, it is difficult to bring about improvements in learning levels on a large scale or sustained basis without working in schools. Partnership with the government at the state level provides the mandate to work in schools. Scaling up has been both easier and quicker in states where Pratham has a partnership (formal or informal) with the state governments. For instance, in Punjab where Pratham has a strong partnership with the state government, the State Project Director of SSA and the Director General of Elementary Education issued a letter to all elementary school headmasters about the launch and objectives of Read Punjab. Also, project management units were set up at the state and district levels. These and other measures allowed Read Punjab to scale up quickly across all districts. On the other hand, in states where Pratham does not have a partnership, the team has to invest a lot of time and energy to convince each government education official at the local level individually about the merits of working with Pratham.

A second advantage of a strong government partnership is that certain activities and their impact are more likely to be sustained in government schools if they are institutionalized and internalized by the system.

Finally, when the government is committed to achieving the goals of the partnership, it typically brings resources to the partnership, both in terms of funds and people. In Punjab, the state government is printing the teaching and learning materials and its people are involved in the training, which reduces the resources that Pratham needs to dedicate to the effort.

ENTRY POINTS FOR WORKING WITH THE GOVERNMENT

Different states have utilized different entry points for working with the government. ASER results have presented a natural entry point for many states: in Punjab, for instance, a meeting between the Pratham team and the state government on the state's ASER results led to a larger discussion on education quality and ultimately, to Read Punjab.

A second approach has been through demonstrating impact. In Chhattisgarh, a state in central India, the state government invited Pratham to do a pilot in one of their toughest districts, Dantewara. The rationale was that if the program could work in the district, it was likely to work anywhere. Dantewara is a district under siege, with a militant group called the Naxalites battling government forces. Most of the population—poor, illiterate, and largely of tribal origin—lives in makeshift camps. Pratham worked with the children in the camp for several months, resulting in a large improvement in learning levels. For instance, the percentage of children who could read letters or less in grades 1 and 2 reduced from 81 to 25 percent. The experience in Dantewada convinced the government about the merits of accepting Pratham's approach and scaling it up in all 18 districts across the state.

In many cases, support from one or more senior government officials has made all the difference. In both Himachal Pradesh and Chhattisgarh, the committed support of a few individuals has played a pivotal role in getting the larger government system to see the merits of a partnership with Pratham.

Occasionally, working with the government has required Pratham to give precedence to the government's goals. For instance, the Bihar government initially decided to focus on enrollment rather than quality of learning. Pratham agreed to invest its resources in Bihar on enrollment. This decision has now paid off: Pratham has established itself in Bihar and developed relationships with various government and non-government agencies. In the process, the issue of quality improvement has slowly seeped into the government's priorities.

NATURE OF PARTNERSHIPS

Pratham's partnerships with state governments take various forms:

- Formal partnership: In states like Bihar and Punjab, formal agreements have been signed with the state governments. These agreements set goals and deadlines and identify roles and responsibilities.
- Strong informal partnership: In states like Chhattisgarh, the state government and Pratham work very closely. Although a formal MoU does not exist, goals are aligned and activities are coordinated with all levels of the government. Also both Pratham and the state SSA machinery jointly monitor and review program implementation.

- Limited partnership: In Uttar Pradesh, although Pratham and the state government have collaborated in all 70 districts in the past, the collaboration has been patchy due to changes at the state leadership level. In other states, like Andhra Pradesh, Maharashtra, and Gujarat, where a state-wide partnership does not exist, Pratham has been working with some government officials at the district and block level.

Typically Pratham provides training to teachers, develops teaching and learning materials, and monitors and evaluates the implementation of the program. In some states and districts, however, only a sub-set of these activities may be followed.

In states where a partnership exists, key government officials have sent out a letter to all government functionaries indicating the rationale of the program and outlining roles and responsibilities.

CHALLENGES OF GOVERNMENT PARTNERSHIPS

While working with the government brings with it several advantages, there are also some challenges that the NGO partner needs to be aware of and prepared for. While partnerships at the state level can open doors across all levels of government, it does not guarantee commitment or ownership at every level. The NGO will still need to make efforts to build support at the district and sub-district levels as well as with relevant government bodies like the District Institutes of Education Training (DIETs). Similarly, a state-level partnership with the government at a particular point of time does not guarantee sustainability. Partnerships can be fragile even when formal agreements are in place—often a change in leadership has changed the nature of partnership. For instance, learning levels improved significantly in Himachal Pradesh in 2007 when there was a strong partnership; however, they dipped again in 2008 when the partnership ended. In this context, creating alignment at all levels of the partnership and a groundswell of grassroots support might ensure greater sustainability. In Bihar, the broad popularity of the "Sankalp" program, a joint initiative of the state government,

Pratham, and UNICEF, has led both the ruling party and the opposition party to publicly announce their enthusiasm for the initiative.

Working with the government can also reduce the flexibility of the program, since the NGO may have to compromise and follow the government's lead in areas like pedagogy, teaching and learning materials, and assessment. Finally, program implementation schedules can be disrupted by inefficiencies or constraints on the government side—for instance, in some states, Pratham has had to step in to distribute materials because the state government did not have an efficient mechanism to do so or step in with its own funds because the release of government funds has been delayed.

APPROACHES IN THE ABSENCE OF GOVERNMENT PARTNERSHIPS

In the absence of partnerships with the state government, Pratham has tried to implement several elements of Read India through several approaches:

- working with the government at the district and block level and with panchayats;
- working with other state departments that have a stake in primary education; and
- working in communities through volunteers.

In Andhra Pradesh, where Pratham currently does not have a partnership with the state unit of SSA, Pratham has followed all three approaches. Pratham's state team has established partnerships with several Mandal Education Officers (a *mandal* is the administration unit at the sub-district level in the state) and panchayats. It is working with the Woman and Child Welfare Department (which implements the Integrated Child Development Services program) and the Adult Literacy Department. Many of the elements of Read India are being implemented in communities through volunteers who are mobilized and trained by Pratham. These volunteers hold classes in their communities in which dedicated time is spent on learning activities and children are provided with access to books and other learning materials.

As mentioned earlier, one of the disadvantages of not having a government partnership is that all costs of implementation have to be borne by the non-profit organization. Pratham has been able to implement an alternative plan in the absence of a state-wide partnership with the government because it has the financial resources to do so—individual and institutional donors from countries across the world have supported Read India.

CONCLUSION

Pratham's partnership with state governments has arguably helped it scale up the Read India program, increased its impact and also improved the chances that the impact will be sustained. At the very least, Pratham's work has helped focus the state and national level governments on the need to focus on learning outcomes. Read India and ASER have essentially changed the paradigm of government partnership in a democracy: instead of people's participation in government programs, we are seeking the government's participation in a people's initiative.

REFERENCES

Department of School Education and Literacy (DoSEL), Government of India. (2010) "1.3 OBJECTIVES OF SARVA SHIKSHA ABHIYAN," in *Sarva Shiksha Abhiyan* (web page). Available online at http://www.education.nic.in/ssa/ssa_1.asp#1.0 (accessed on 4 May 2010).

ASER Centre. (2010) "ASER 2005 Data." Available online at http://asercentre.org/asersurvey/aser05.php (accessed on 4 May 2010).

C H A P T E R 5

Social Entrepreneurship across National Boundaries

Behzad J. Larry, Azad Oommen,
and *Venkatesh "Venky" Raghavendra*

Entrepreneurial drive is the common denominator for the American India Foundation (AIF) and The Indus Entrepreneurs (TiE). Operating in parallel spheres of business and development, the missions of the two organizations overlap in the process of promoting entrepreneurship.

This chapter highlights the shared vision of AIF and TiE-Boston, and demonstrates how social endeavors can cross national boundaries and have significant impact on both sides despite the distance between them.

While TiE has been a much-vaunted networking model for business entrepreneurs, AIF has developed a strong network of social entrepreneurs in India and philanthropic entrepreneurs in the United States. AIF's philanthropic community is passionate about India and works toward improving the socioeconomic conditions in India in the areas of education, livelihood, and public health. The AIF chapter in Boston was created in 2001, and over the course of the years has become a strong presence in the community with many of its efforts driven by members of TiE-Boston.

Over the years TiE-Boston and AIF have worked closely to achieve common goals in education—such as access to education for under-privileged children, livelihood, income generation opportunities for the youth, and public health to provide better health care for everyone. We continue to build on that and deepen our relationships to engage the TiE community in the philanthropic initiatives of AIF in India.

THE GENESIS OF AIF

In the wake of the 2001 Gujarat earthquake in India, President Bill Clinton joined hands with leaders of the Indian diaspora in America and corporate leaders with an interest in India to create the American India Foundation. AIF raised over $4 million for relief and rehabilitation in Gujarat. Seeing a niche of a strategic philanthropy focused exclusively on India, AIF expanded its work to other parts of the country and is now focused on India's education, livelihood, and health care sectors.

Today, AIF is a non-profit organization that is devoted to cata-lyzing social and economic change in India. AIF has invested in over 100 Indian non-governmental organizations (NGOs) while raising over $50 million since its inception. It is one of the largest secular, non-partisan American organizations supporting development work exclusively in India.

AIF'S WORKING PARADIGM

Modeling the best practices of entrepreneurial organizations in the private sector, AIF has developed an operational approach that is strategic, leveraged, and geared toward acting as a catalyst for change in India (Figure 5.1).

FIGURE 5.1 AIF's Working Paradigm

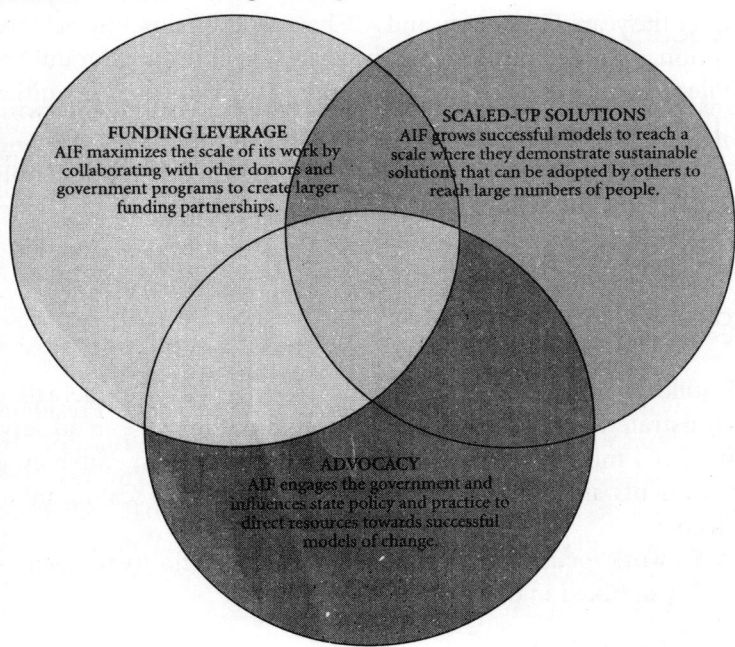

Source: AIF.

Funding Leverage

The development sector in India can be a confusing landscape for donors who wish to contribute to change. With over 100,000 NGOs registered in India, it is difficult to determine where to make a charitable contribution. AIF is an easy and effective way for donors to make thoughtful investments into organizations that are monitored for their progress. In addition, because donors' resources are pooled together to make investments, they are able to make a difference on a scale that would be difficult to achieve individually.

Advocacy

Transformational change occurs when governments partner with civil society to adopt policies based on impactful models. AIF and its partners have influenced policy at the national and state levels by demonstrating successful models of change.

Scale

AIF builds models from small pilot investments to a scale where they demonstrate the potential for triggering broad change in society. Many such models are delivering exceptional results, convincing governments and other donor agencies to continue scaling these projects.

AIF's work focuses on three broad programmatic areas. Each of these is examined in detail next.

EDUCATION—INCREASING ACCESS AND EMPOWERMENT

AIF's approach to working in the area of elementary education is premised on the fact that it is the state's responsibility to fulfill its constitutional mandate of free and compulsory education for all children between 6 and 14 years of age, and that the Government of India has committed itself to the Universalization of Elementary Education (UEE) by 2010.

AIF's education programs, therefore, focus on complementing and supplementing state efforts in meeting the commitments. It does this by working with partner NGOs that focus on the "left-out children" and finds ways to ensure that such children have access to quality education, and are able to successfully complete the primary and the elementary education. AIF works with the children of seasonal migrants and deprived urban children who are excluded due to reasons of social stigma.

In these groups, the focus is on the girl child, and children of ethnic/religious minorities, while work is continued on improving the quality of education, and strengthening government schools. Currently AIF has eight partners in education, six in the area of seasonal migration and two in the area of deprived urban children. Some of the partners include Janarth, Setu, and Bodh.

Learning and Migration Program: A Flagship Program within AIF's Education Pillar Addressing the Migrant Population and Their Children's Education

An estimated six million children migrate with their parents seasonally and most drop out of school during the migration period, impeding their continued education. With AIF's Learning and Migration Program (LAMP), partners are now directly educating around 30,000 children every year, and concerted advocacy efforts have moved the government to support and scale up these models of education. This has resulted in a significant increase in the number of children being educated.

The migrant's children accompany them because there is no option to leave them behind in their villages. When given a safe and nurturing environment in which to leave their children, such as the seasonal hostels run by AIF, parents are eager to spare their children the hardship of migration. In working with people living with HIV/AIDS or at risk of the disease, AIF is reaching out to those who face frequent discrimination. In fact, many people do not even get tested because medical care is rarely available to them and they would face the added burden of discrimination if they are found to be HIV-positive. By educating people about the disease, encouraging HIV-testing, and connecting HIV patients to treatment facilities, AIF is making life better for people with little hope.

The Government of India's Sarva Shiksha Abhiyan (Universal Elementary Education) program has notified all states to identify and include children whose education is affected due to migration. The governments of Gujarat, Maharashtra, and Orissa have committed to supporting and replicating seasonal hostels pioneered by AIF. In the 2008–09 school year, they are investing $12.5 million to educate 145,000 children affected by migration.

Also this year, the Andhra Pradesh government partnered with six AIF-supported NGOs in Hyderabad to provide education to 26,000 children of construction workers. This is the first LAMP site benefiting migrant children in an urban environment.

PHOTOGRAPH 5.1 Seasonal Hostel for boys, Yusuf Meherally Center, Kutch, Gujarat

Source: AIF, © Prashant Panjiar.

Digital Equalizer: Addressing Issues of Digital Divide

AIF's Digital Equalizer (DE) program enables thousands of children in under-resourced schools to incorporate digital technology into their education and become better prepared to be part of the

21st century workforce. Designed for grades 6 through 10 (ages 10–14), a DE center is supported by AIF in a school for 3 years, and most function independently thereafter. The DE program has had a remarkable growth path. Beginning with 49 schools in 2001–02, it has grown to 1,500 schools in 2008–09, enhancing the quality of education of over 600,000 children and 16,000 teachers. In its first three years, DE operated mostly through investments of private individuals and corporations. AIF spent this time fine-tuning the model and demonstrating its success. However, rapid expansion was needed to enable the millions of children who had never experienced technology as part of their education to catch up with the rest of the world.

AIF's investment in the DE model bore fruit when state governments began to partner with it to grow the program. Punjab, Andhra Pradesh, Orissa, Karnataka, and Rajasthan invested in the infrastructure needed to set up and operate DE centers and AIF provided the training and ongoing operational support. For the 2008–09 school year, AIF has added a partnership with the government of Tamil Nadu to implement DE in 150 schools in the coastal areas impacted by the 2004 tsunami.

AIF is now achieving the same impact as earlier at 1/10th of the cost. Now, corporate partners are providing DE the capital to innovate and enhance its model, and expand into new geographies. The Adobe Youth Voices project has doubled its reach and is now available at 25 schools, reaching 700 students, helping them learn how to use digital media to highlight social issues in their communities.

PUBLIC HEALTH: FURTHERING MATERNAL AND CHILD HEALTH CARE

Guided by national priorities, AIF is rolling out a new generation of programs under its Public Health portfolio, with a focus on building community investment and ownership. The goal of the program is

PHOTOGRAPH 5.2   Students Take Turns Experiencing Digital Learning in the Classroom. Digital Equalizer, Rajasthan

Source: AIF, © Prashant Panjiar.

to reduce mortality and the burden of disease in impoverished and under-served communities by promoting and protecting healthy lifestyles.

The emphasis will be on accelerating health literacy, particularly about preventable and infectious diseases, and strengthening health systems for delivery of quality services. AIF's interventions will bring private sector resources and ingenuity to drive public health changes for saving lives, particularly those of women and children.

Apna Klinic

The objective of Apna Klinic is to build a replicable model of an urban health center for sustained improvement in Reproductive, Maternal and Child Health (RMCH) in the slums of Delhi. It is expected that the project would cater to the RMCH needs of approximately 50,000 to 60,000 people in the area. Some of the proposed interventions are preventive and curative services to pregnant women and children below six years—three antenatal care check-ups, two tetanus toxoid immunizations, iron and folic acid supplementation and counseling on birth preparedness, maternal and neonatal danger sign recognition and early initiation of breast feeding, intra-partum and post-partum care, and infant care. It provides curative services to men and women suffering from reproductive illness and/or sexually transmitted disease, counseling and family planning services, immunization, and basic sanitation.

LIVELIHOOD: CREATING ECONOMIC OPPORTUNITIES TO BUILD SOCIAL EQUITY

In rural areas, AIF concentrates on those geographies and constituencies that are characterized by being chronically drought prone, undulating topography, an acute degradation of natural resources, semi-arid climatic conditions, and afflicted by shortages of drinking water. In these places, even in years of adequate rainfall, crop distress is caused by the gaps in the rain at critical points of time in the crop growth cycle.

In urban areas, AIF's work priorities go beyond large metro cities, that is, focus on medium and small towns from poorer states in northern and eastern India. Urban population growth is much higher than the rate of overall population growth, and currently an estimated 29 percent of India's population lives in urban areas.

AIF's approach is to link the urban poor and migrants with various types of self-employment and wage employment opportunities that are emerging in an urban informal sector economy. This is achieved by taking full advantage of the growing economy, mainly around the services, manufacturing, and construction sectors. AIF partners accomplish this mainly by forming collectives, promoting saving and credit groups, training and exposure to vocational skills, linking them up with markets, and promoting group enterprises. Forming groups or collectives of urban poor enable them to better negotiate their terms of engagement. Some of the urban poor who have been mobilized for livelihood enhancement are construction workers, rickshaw pullers, home managers, rag pickers and sweepers, etc.

In the *safai mitra* (friends of cleanliness) livelihood program implemented in partnership with Nidan in Bihar, AIF is enabling waste collectors and rag pickers to become business owners through their collective ownership of the Swachdhara, a waste management enterprise. Among the urban poor, collecting waste from the streets is one of the most immediately accessible jobs, but also one fraught with danger, discrimination, and a total lack of income security. Those engaged in this profession are at the bottom of the economic ladder. By being part of a professionally organized business, they gain an employment with dignity and income security.

PHOTOGRAPH 5.3   *Safai Mitra* (Friends of Cleanliness) Organize into a Collective for Dignified and Regular Employment

Source: AIF, © Prashant Panjiar.

Within the boundaries of its three program areas, AIF provides financial and technical support to its partner organizations, and also advocates with the governments for effective policy creation. Two means of support from AIF that are highlighted in the following pages are the Service Corps Fellowship and Disaster Relief Assistance.

Service Corps Fellowship: An Influx of Youthful, Creative Energy into Civil Society, and Leadership Development

This program helps to build bridges between America and India by sending young, talented, and skilled Americans to work with leading NGOs in India for a period of 10 months. The program serves as an exchange of technical skills and intellectual resources, and aims to build the capacity of Indian NGOs while developing American leaders with an understanding of India.

The AIF Service Corps Fellowship was born from the high level of interest expressed by young Americans to assist in the post-earthquake rehabilitation of Gujarat in 2001. Beginning with a pilot class of 21 fellows in 2001, the program has now sent 169 Fellows to 74 organizations throughout India. This experience enables the fellows to understand and make a deep impact in the development sector by working at grassroots level with various NGOs, who are striving to advance social and economic change in India.

The Service Corps Fellows, who stem from diverse educational and professional backgrounds, come together in their common desire to help unearth India's potential and are willing to challenge themselves on all levels to achieve this goal. The Gandhian essence of the Fellowship calls upon a sense of commitment and self-reliance in its fellows as well as a deep desire to help others empower themselves.

Nalini Sharma, a founding member of the Boston AIF Leadership Council, was recently involved in the selection process of the Service Corps Fellows. She interviewed a number of candidates in Boston and had this to say:

I had the privilege and pleasure of interviewing several candidates for the AIF Service Corps Fellowship program. It was an intellectually stimulating and, at the same time, a humbling experience. It makes the selection process a very difficult one! The candidates were uniformly accomplished, highly qualified and deeply committed individuals. The fact that the Service Corp fellowship program attracts candidates of this caliber is a true testament to AIF's own commitment to make a difference through its programs. Once again, I have witnessed first hand, the transformative ability of AIF in the field of service and philanthropy in India. Knowing that these young, dedicated Americans will take on the reins of leadership tomorrow with such a commitment to India is truly heart warming.

Disaster Relief: Support in Times of Distress and Calamity

Disaster relief work, with which AIF originally started, continues to be a strong focus area for the organization. Responding to the catastrophe of Tsunami in 2004, the American India Foundation established the Tsunami Relief Fund and raised over $2 million for the victims in India. AIF focused on two of the worst affected regions, Tamil Nadu and the Andaman and Nicobar Islands. In partnership with the United Nations Development Programme (UNDP), AIF also supported work in Kerala. AIF's work in the Andamans was limited because of a dearth of reliable NGOs working there and as the Government of India had a very strong role in determining what interventions took place.

The bulk of AIF's support went to non-fishing communities, which included farmers, petty traders, and salt pan workers, as they were left out of most interventions, either because of their caste or the general focus on the fishing communities, whose livelihood was extensively damaged. The limited resources available to the other communities made them extremely vulnerable.

AIF's intervention at the relief phase was minimal due to its limited presence in the affected areas and the swift and significant response of the government. AIF restricted itself to areas that did not receive adequate relief. It stayed out of activities like housing and provision of fishing boats and nets because this required huge investments and the efforts of the government and large inter-national agencies were concentrated here. Though AIF wished to intervene in education, there was little need as most schools were intact and hence restricted itself to pre-primary education and establishing digital equalizer centers.

In the four years since the disaster, AIF has made a significant amount of progress. Its rehabilitation work is making a difference in the lives of many tsunami victims; however, long-term rehabilitation requires continued dedication in the years ahead. Therefore, AIF will continue to closely monitor the projects it has funded in order to ensure complete success.

AIF'S US CHAPTERS

AIF has chapters in various cities across the United States. Most of the chapters are concentrated in cities with large Indian population as well as cities where there are many Indian centric companies. The chapters function in two main areas, first, they build awareness about AIF's work and India's social issues. Second, they are also a source of generating resources. 2007–08 saw the emergence of the Boston chapter, which raised $300,000 at its inaugural fundraiser. The Los Angeles chapter, in a gala underwritten by the Bill and Melinda Gates Foundation, raised nearly $1 million. The Chicago chapter, in its third annual gala, raised $750,000. The New York and Bay Area galas continued to lead the way, raisings $3 million and $2 million respectively. Together, the chapters are a physical representation of the collective spirit of giving that AIF seeks to foster. Donors across the country pooling together their resources results in an expanded pie to be invested in India and a more stable funding base for the organization.

LEADERSHIP TRIPS AND SITE VISITS

One of the best and the strongest ways of understanding the issues in India, and the work AIF is involved in, is by paying a visit to these areas and seeing them first hand. Several TiE-Boston members have taken the initiative to visit India and see the ongoing work. This helps them to connect to these causes and the projects on a more personal basis. It also helps them see the fruitions of their commitment to AIF.

An Interaction That Endeared Them to AIF's Mission

Raj and Nalini Sharma, TiE members from Boston, chaired the AIF's first annual benefit gala in Boston. A turning point for them in their association with AIF was the site visits they did in Hyderabad, Andhra Pradesh. Here, Raj and Nalini have shared their experience:

> We would like to share with you our own personal experience with AIF. In 2004, Nalini, our children, and myself had the opportunity to visit a government school for girls in our hometown of Hyderabad to witness AIF's Digital Equalizer program in action. We were thoroughly impressed by the design of the program, and in particular, the computers, Internet access and training that AIF provided.
>
> However, what really took our breath away was the visible optimism on the faces of the children, mostly drawn from economically disadvantaged families. AIF gave these children the ability to dream … a prism to see the outside world and showed them the promise of a better future. This is only one mere example. There are numerous stories of success for AIF all over the country in areas such as primary education for children of migrant workers, women's empowerment and health care. India is a land with unlimited potential and promise and at the same time, millions of children are left behind. AIF is their beacon of hope.
>
> It is an open, transparent organization that has the potential to make a major impact on the social and economic landscape in India by engaging the Indian Diaspora and well-wishers around the world.

Daughter of Bihar Makes a Connection!

TiE member Reema Chandra recently went on one of AIF's leadership tours as well. She shared her thoughts from her trip:

> When I landed at Patna airport it felt like I had come home after a long journey. On the surface it seemed that not much had changed in the 15 years since I left Bihar. Riding from the airport on roads in decrepit condition left me wondering about so many questions: When, where and what went wrong with Bihar? Why could it not participate in the torrid GDP growth rate that rest of the India is experiencing? Who could make that happen and how?

My husband Amitabh and I grew up in Bihar before it was bifurcated into two states and we feel we have Bihar and Jharkhand living in us together as one. While these states have illustrious histories, Bihar is now also a state where not enough growth and progress have entered the lives of ordinary citizens for some years.

To my pleasant surprise, my questions and concerns were partially answered by an enthusiastic welcome at the official residence of Chief Minister of Bihar, Mr. Nitish Kumar. It was heartening to hear how genuine and humble Mr Kumar sounded. He believes in making basic health care and primary education available to the people of Bihar, he advocates empowerment of women, and he realizes that the Bihar government has a difficult road ahead for bringing development and growth in the state. However, he looked ready to tackle these hurdles. He actively voiced his support for AIF's work in Bihar.

A similar level of commitment to growth in Bihar was evident at a reception in Patna that Amitabh and I hosted. Along with our NGO partners, the guest list spanned from the Energy minister, Urban Development minister, the mayor of Patna to representatives from Bihar state AIDS Control Society, International Health Organization and UNICEF. This change in attitude amongst the bureaucrats was quite different from what I had known fifteen years ago. I had finally found at least one reason to start hoping that Bihar and Jharkhand could again be counted among the best-governed states in India.

AIF's partnership with MAMTA for strengthening the existing health care system provided by state health centers, and with Nidan for organizing waste collectors into worker-owned collectives to have access to a secure livelihood and worker benefits, provide answers to some of the "who?" and "how?" questions that had given me an uneasy feeling.

My visit to the MAMTA project at Phulvarisharif (an hour outside of Patna) was a mixture of apprehensions, concerns, emotions and results. Cheerful greetings by kids, shy smiles of women and honest answers by men were all part of an experience that is hard to describe in words. It seemed that being a woman myself and also being a "Bihari," women had an instant connection with me. They were so eager to share their vision and stories of their lives. One of them shared at great lengths about her homegrown health center and providing protective measures for safe-sex practices to the women of the village as well the neighboring ones. I left with one thought—so many questions to be answered, and so much more to be done.

The next morning I found the same zeal and attitude in the minds of street sweepers (*safai mitra*), the beneficiaries of Nidan. The *safai mitras* work as contractors for the city government to manage household waste. Through a recycling and a vermi-composting site, they have been putting their entrepreneurial skills to use in generating additional revenues. I kept wondering at the small but justified need that we, as people on the other side of the track, can fulfill to help them reach their goals. This time I left that vast gathering of *safai mitras* and their families with hopes and determination that it is possible for these people to have a better life for them, and we can help to make it happen.

I am now back home in Boston with Amitabh and our children, Neil and Aeshna, and I often slip back in the lanes of Patna trying to visualize those moments again, feeling a sense of pride in those words when women in Phulvarisharif called me "daughter of Bihar" and becoming even more resolute in being there for them in their struggle for a better life. I invite you to join me in this journey.

AIF Leadership Tour Report: An Economist's Perspective

Ravi Mantha, another TiE member, wrote this about his recent visit to AIF sites around India:

When I was invited to attend the AIF leadership trip this year, I was delighted but apprehensive. Having been a donor for the past two years, I still had a fundamental question about whether AIF addresses a core need in India or simply creates demand for its services by providing a source of cash. Charity is a complex field, and I had some prior experience of the pitfalls of giving without regard for process.

Eighteen years ago, as a college student with an interest in development economics, I spent an afternoon outside the busy Shanbagh Café in Hyderabad, measuring the response rate of a small band of panhandlers soliciting alms at the intersection.

Six panhandlers worked the stoplights ceaselessly in the searing heat of the June sun. They were all employees of the local street boss, and were paid a fixed rate between ten and fifteen rupees a day (based on age, not takings) plus free food. Their receipts went straight into the pocket of the local goonda, who paid around half of the proceeds to the local politician who then made sure the activity was not disturbed, and so on.

My experiment found a gullible donor rate of around four percent, with each beggar grossing about a hundred rupees in a ten-hour workday. My conclusion was that street level begging in urban India is largely a supply-driven force, stemming from the impulse charity urges of a small minority of people stopped at traffic lights, even though it annoys the other 96% who do not wish to be accosted.

It will not surprise you to know that when I was invited to participate in the AIF leadership trip, I packed an extra-large suitcase filled with the cynicism that has only grown in the years since my experiment.

Our first AIF visit was to a school in Chennai, which hosted a Digital Equalizer (DE) Center. By providing computer-aided learning to under-resourced schools, AIF ensures that future generations of Indians are part of the digital age regardless of their economic status. Simply brilliant! The key finding for me was that whenever schools take part in DE, parents compete to send their kids there, and neighboring schools are goaded into trying to take part in DE as well. A virtuous cycle of competition by schools is exactly what urban India needs to take education to the next level.

Our next stop was an AIDS hospital. After years of bad news, the story of AIDS in India has finally turned the corner. Prevention efforts are starting to work, and the social stigma associated with HIV has begun to weaken. But we cannot afford to relax, as India still has more HIV cases than any other country in the world, and managing the health of these individuals is an essential task.

Before we bid adieu to Tamil Nadu, we had a look in at a dairy cooperative for women who had been affected by the tsunami in rural Cuddalore District. Here AIF's contribution enabled village women to buy a pair of cows and create a women-owned milk enterprise so they would have year-round income from milk sales. These women now run a dairy enterprise, with a milk chilling and transportation center. Escorted into a big thatched hut we were treated to tea and individual stories of lives altered by a newfound sense of community and a can-do attitude, all from a small loan.

In Andhra Pradesh, we spent time in an HIV clinic with orphan children, some of whom were also HIV positive. It was truly the most heartening part of the trip to see that these kids not only have hope but also can expect a more or less normal life thanks to AIF and its partner organizations.

It took me a while to put this all into perspective; to take a step back from the often emotional stories of real people in need that were in front of us daily, and to look at the broader picture. And here I come to the last and the most important part of my findings; the reason I will continue to support AIF.

In a very broad sense, charity dollars can be spent on two main noble causes; prevention and compassion. Many of the larger and better-known foundations focus exclusively on prevention, the best example of this being the Bill and Melinda Gates Foundation. In AIF, though, I find an organization that appeals to both my mind and my heart. It is addressing problems not only from a strategic prevention perspective, but it is actively engaged in compassion; enabling people who are suffering today to lead a better life.

When we went to the AIDS hospitals in Chennai and Andhra Pradesh, it was apparent to me that the angels devoted to helping patients deserved every dollar of support from us. When we went to a school for migrant workers in Hyderabad and saw AIF's efforts to get migrant kids into the education net, it became clear to me that we cannot treat even a single child as part of a so-called lost generation.

Economics may teach us about being efficient, and from an economics standpoint prevention is always better than cure because limited resources can be leveraged to go a lot further. But our social contract with our fellow human beings is forged with our hearts, and the language of the heart is written in love and compassion, not economics. Striking an equitable balance between prevention and compassion with charity resources is therefore hugely important, and this is where AIF is showing the way forward.

So many others share Mr Mantha's earlier doubts and skepticisms about the efficiencies of charitable work. Yet these melt away upon witnessing the capable network created by AIF. Money invested in NGOs provides countless underprivileged Indians the opportunity to earn a livelihood, advance their education, or simply to live better lives in a sustainable manner.

Seeing Is Believing!

Venkat Srinivasan who was also on the same trip as Ravi Mantha shared excerpts from his India trip. Here are some of his anecdotes:

We visited a school, attended mostly by children from nearby slums, with a Digital Equalizer (DE) center in Chennai... We met with a number of the children who were using the computer lab that AIF has supported as part of the DE program. Having gone to a similar (government) school myself, I could readily relate to the environment and it brought back a lot of memories. It was wonderful to see the gratitude in those kids' eyes and their appreciation toward AIF for having made a big difference in their lives.

We even met one alum who is currently pursuing a Ph.D. program in Chennai!

We then visited YRGCare (founded by Dr Solomon), which is a full-fledged hospital providing HIV detection, treatment and research. Starting with a make-shift hut with a thatched roof when no hospital would admit HIV patients, YRGCare has grown into a full fledged, internationally recognized HIV/AIDS hospital today. They work with Yale, Brown, WHO and other international institutions and conduct clinical and other research related to AIDS in addition to their detecton and treatment programs.

At lunch, we met with students who had graduated in vocational training programs provided by another NGO. These students were from very poor families and really had no access to formal education. It was great to hear the aspirations of these young people who clearly now have acquired meaningful skills.

We flew to Hyderabad and went to an AIDS orphanage called the Desire Society in Medak district. It was heart breaking to see little children who were all HIV+, many of whom were orphans. We came to grips with the ground realities—the difficulty of detecting the presence of HIV due to the social stigma. This society had set up a community health center in the main village and provided general medical treatment to the village in the hope that it can convince many patients to undergo confidential HIV screening. YRGCare from Chennai provides the training to doctors in this facility.

AIF had organized a seminar on "urban migration" and along with its partners, YES Bank and USIBC, released a knowledge paper on the issue. The intent was to bring the urban migration issue to the forefront of senior planners and bureaucrats. We had an interesting set of panelists who presented a broad range of views ranging from the magnitude of the issue to the critical role of urban planning in managing rural to urban migration. Present were senior government bureaucrats including a member of the Planning Commission. I thought the idea of a seminar focused on topical developmental issues where AIF has a position and practical results was a terrific idea.

CONCLUSION

This chapter is a case in how organizations can tap one community to help another, even when the two communities are geographically distant. It also highlights the power of collective philanthropy.

AIF has succeeded in creating the enabling environment for giving to India. It has also shown that there is more power in giving together and pooling resources in order to have a greater impact on the ground. In this regard, the alignment of values between AIF and TiE has helped them come together in various locations including Boston. Together the two organizations have not only channeled financial resources but also transferred human resources and good ideas to energize the various social-change efforts in India.

CHAPTER 6

The Evolution of Ubuntu at Work: Helping Women Micro Entrepreneurs Escape the Poverty Trap

Vibha Pingle

THE ROOTS

In almost every developing country for which there is detailed survey data available, nearly 50 percent of the urban population and much more than 50 percent of the rural population run micro enterprises and live on less than $2 a day. This suggests that one strategy for reducing poverty would be to help micro entrepreneurs develop their businesses.

Ubuntu at Work, Inc., the global non-profit for assisting women micro entrepreneurs, emerged out of research I conducted on micro entrepreneurship in South Africa a few years ago. My research project sought to answer a key question: why are some women micro entrepreneurs successful at developing their micro enterprise while others are not? I was interested in exploring what kinds of social capital helped some women micro entrepreneurs transform their struggling micro enterprises into successful ones thus escaping the poverty trap.

To answer these questions I spent over a year in South Africa talking to women micro entrepreneurs across the country. My conversations were unstructured and informal. I met the women at their homes or micro enterprises. In subsequent research projects I had similar conversations with women micro entrepreneurs in Egypt, northern Nigeria, Nepal, Indonesia, and India.

The results of my study were startling. Contrary to conventional ideas about the value of self-help groups for assisting micro entrepreneurs, they showed that women micro entrepreneurs who were connected to extra-local networks were much more successful than women micro entrepreneurs only connected to local community networks and self-help groups.

Further investigations revealed that the women micro entrepreneurs connected to extra-local networks had been thus connected serendipitously—for example, a tourist walking by had connected one women micro entrepreneur to an international non-profit, and in another instance, a researcher had connected a woman micro entrepreneur to a national craft producer and retailer. Ubuntu at Work seeks to make extra-local connections systematically available to women micro entrepreneurs.

My research also indicated that women micro entrepreneurs tend not to see themselves as businesswomen. They see themselves primarily as mothers, wives, and daughters, not as businesswomen. They consider running a small business as what they have to do to provide food for their family. Consequently, they often do not take advantage of opportunities for learning business skills (such as government-funded training programs) that might be available to them.

So how can we systematically connect women micro entrepreneurs to extra-local networks and help them identify business opportunities? How can we present these opportunities and assistance to women micro entrepreneurs such that they see the opportunities resonating with their lives and their identities as mothers, daughters, and wives?

THE CORE IDEA

Ubuntu at Work is a social networking platform that brings together women micro entrepreneurs with professionals, artists, designers, fair trade retailers, educators, public health educators, etc. Ubuntu at Work leverages the power of social networking technologies to help women micro entrepreneurs escape poverty. It connects women micro entrepreneurs across developing countries with coaches to help them with their businesses. Ubuntu at Work coaches help women micro entrepreneurs develop business ideas, identify funding sources, and draw on global resources. Coaches help women micro entrepreneurs transform their businesses from survivalist to entrepreneurial entities, thus escaping poverty. Since women micro entrepreneurs see their enterprise as integrated into their family life, our coaching is holistic.

Our logo is inspired by Warli art from western India and Maori art from New Zealand. The spiral, or the "Koru" as it is known in Maori, is symbolic of the opening of a tree fern frond, representing the awakening of new life, positive change, and personal growth (http://ubuntuatwork.org). Our name, Ubuntu at Work, translates into humanity or community at work. Ubuntu is a southern African philosophical concept according to which "I am because we are." Like our logo and name we bring resources, ideas, energy, and enthusiasm from the far reaches of the world to form a community that helps women escape poverty.

Ubuntu at Work coaching is done via our social networking website (Figure 6.1). Since most women micro entrepreneurs are not computer literate, partner microfinance institution (MFI) staff and Ubuntu at Work staff/volunteers communicate the coaching conversations to the women micro entrepreneurs. With coaching from Ubuntu at Work's global social networking community,

FIGURE 6.1 The Ubuntu at Work Social Networking Community: A High-level Perspective

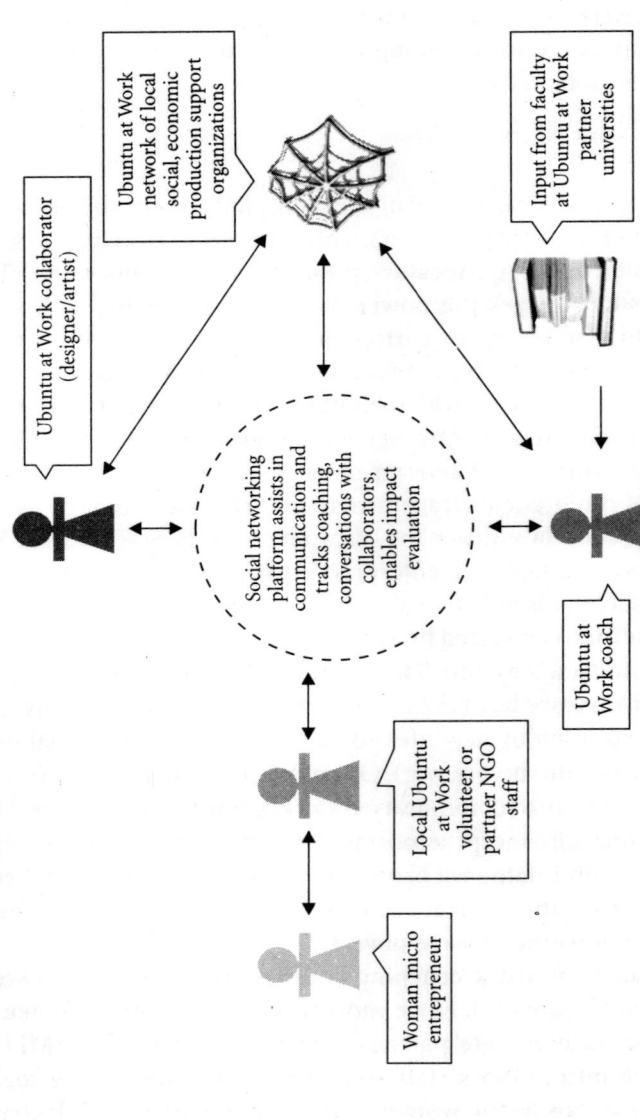

Ubuntu at Work collaborator (designer/artist)

Ubuntu at Work network of local social, economic production support organizations

Input from faculty at Ubuntu at Work partner universities

Social networking platform assists in communication and tracks coaching, conversations with collaborators, enables impact evaluation

Ubuntu at Work coach

Local Ubuntu at Work volunteer or partner NGO staff

Woman micro entrepreneur

Source: Ubuntu at Work, Inc.

women micro entrepreneurs are better able to: use microfinance in a strategic and entrepreneurial manner; develop sustainable micro enterprises; and accumulate assets. Ubuntu at Work target beneficiaries are from among the most vulnerable demographic segments globally.

THE JOURNEY

Translating my initial research conclusions into practical initiatives that would lead to the formation of Ubuntu at Work has been a long and convoluted journey. Ubuntu at Work began evolving soon after I completed my research in South Africa.

As I left South Africa and returned to the United States I knew I wanted to find a way of giving back to the women micro entrepreneurs who had shared their stories with me. I began thinking about starting a non-profit, but was rather unsure of how I would go about it. As an academic I had had little experience with getting a start-up off the ground. I was a lot more comfortable with assisting women micro entrepreneurs by provoking an academic debate around development issues.

Questions of women's identity and what leads some women micro entrepreneurs to think entrepreneurially began to absorb me. The more time I spent reading and reflecting on questions of identity, the further away I got from doing anything practical to help women micro entrepreneurs succeed in escaping poverty. Return visits to South Africa to meet my interviewees and interlocutors only made me more conscious of the chasm between where my arguments about identity were taking me and where the women wanted to be and how I could assist them.

If starting a non-profit seemed impossible, exploring policies that might be useful for assisting women micro entrepreneurs and contributing to policy debates seemed like a promising route. A visit to Ghana on a policy-consulting assignment led me to explore the experience of women micro entrepreneurs elsewhere in Africa and the kinds of policies that might assist them.

Working on economic and social policies seemed like a good way to develop the policy implications of my South African research. It had the added advantage of helping me gradually transition out of academia and into what non-academics call the "real" world. Thinking along these lines I joined a development think-tank in the UK. I had hoped that my experience there would help me get closer to my goal of starting a non-profit to assist women micro entrepreneurs.

As a development consultant I spent time in Egypt, northern Nigeria, Nepal, and Indonesia. While in these countries I interviewed women micro entrepreneurs. In Egypt I interviewed women micro entrepreneurs in one of Cairo's largest slums, in the smaller towns of Minya, and in villages along the Nile. Their responses were strikingly similar to those of women micro entrepreneurs in South Africa. The very significant differences in historical experiences, culture, and religion appear to have little noticeable impact on how women micro entrepreneurs define themselves, view their enterprises, or are able to successfully develop them.

Interviews with women micro entrepreneurs in northern Nigeria's provinces of Kano and Katsina offered further evidence in support of this conclusion; as did subsequent interviews in Nepal, Indonesia, and India. The data I gathered from these six countries, three in Asia and three in Africa, all suggested that one way to help women micro entrepreneurs escape poverty is to connect them to extra-local networks that assist them in exploring new business opportunities and offer support for taking advantage of these opportunities.

LAUNCHING UBUNTU AT WORK

Building a Partner Network

Ubuntu at Work is developing a network of partner MFIs and universities. Women micro entrepreneurs, clients of these MFIs, participate in online conversations with coaches. Coaches are recruited from among professionals in the Ubuntu at Work community and from among graduate students at Ubuntu at Work's partner universities. Coaches receive Ubuntu at Work training/tools for coaching women micro entrepreneurs.

Before launching Ubuntu at Work in the fall of 2009, I contacted the heads of two MFIs—one in Cairo and one in Bangalore. During the course of my research into micro entrepreneurship I had interviewed women micro entrepreneurs who were clients of these MFIs. Their enthusiastic support of the idea at the core of Ubuntu at Work was very important and definitely helped me move forward.

My next step was to reach out to former colleagues and friends who might be interested in joining me in creating Ubuntu at Work. Ubuntu at Work currently has four core team members. This includes: Anne Marie Duffy, who spent over 10 years as a senior executive at a large boutique financial services firm in Boston; Matthew Rudolph, a political scientist who has extensive understanding of emerging market financial sectors; and Roohia Sidhu Klein, a corporate attorney with global experience. The four of us are involved in the daily operations of Ubuntu at Work Inc. In India, a sole staff person, Basavaraj Kalaveeappanavar, coordinates a team of volunteers led by Smita Chakravorty, and with their help manages our various India initiatives.

In addition our development committee, a team of experts in relevant areas, advises us on our strategy and our operations. Included in the development committee are: Guy Stuart, a professor at the Kennedy School of Government at Harvard University; Vijayendra Rao, Lead Economist at the World Bank; Karim Lakhani, a professor at Harvard Business School; Ashutosh Varshney, a professor at Brown University; and Catherine Kerr, a professor at Harvard Medical School.

We have had teams of students from Boston University's Business School develop the business case for our microfinance and jewelry production initiatives. Plus, we have a growing army of volunteers scattered around the world helping us with fundraising, developing our coaching modules, collaboratively designing green products that women can produce, website development, and marketing our products.

Developing the Social Networking Platform

With extensive help from our volunteers, Ubuntu at Work has created a social networking website that enables our coaching conversations. Since women micro entrepreneurs are not computer literate, MFI/Ubuntu at Work volunteers assist in the coaching conversations. Our volunteers convey messages between women micro entrepreneurs and coaches. Where possible mobile telephony is used to enhance this communication.

We began developing our website and our social networking site last fall. My goal was to create a social networking platform that would allow us to communicate with our MFI partners and their women micro entrepreneur clients. We were thrilled to have experienced web developers, many our own volunteers, create our platform for us pro bono. After internal discussions and consultations with our MFI partners we identified core functionalities the social networking site was to have. The process was time consuming, but ultimately successful.

While our social networking platform was under development, we began using Facebook to reach volunteers/supporters, potential coaches, and to begin developing an online Ubuntu at Work community. With help from volunteers we created a "cause" and a "fan" page on Facebook that became the virtual home of our online community. It became a forum in which our volunteers were able to participate and contribute. Finally, it allowed us to understand both the limitations and the advantages of having an online community and the opportunities it offers us as we develop.

The Coaching Process

At the same time as Ubuntu at Work began creating partnerships with MFIs and developing a social networking platform, we also began formalizing our coaching process and toolkit. Formalizing the coaching process meant that we had to define our coaching philosophy and pedagogy.

Our coaching approach:

- Coaching is a partnership used to discuss problems and solve issues and challenges and to provide support and guidance for the achievement of agreed-upon goals.
- A coach supports and holds the women micro entrepreneurs' agenda so as to focus on their vision and goals, and limit distractions that interfere with accomplishing objectives.
- Coaching facilitates goal achievement by clarifying values, brainstorming, developing action plans, examining modes of operation, making empowering requests, and providing structures and accountability.

Coaching steps:

- "Enrolling" in coaching

  (a) Women micro entrepreneurs are informed about Ubuntu at Work and invited to participate in our coaching conversations.
  (b) Women micro entrepreneurs express a willingness to work honestly and candidly with the coach.
  (c) Upon their acceptance, we discuss mutual goals, the logistics of the coaching process, and develop a tentative action plan.
- Engagement

  (a) Starting the relationship/building trust.
  (b) Set the parameters: confidentiality, how information will be used, how long will we work together, etc.
- Data gathering

  (a) Current situation and challenges, past experiences, and life circumstances.
  (b) Personal history, including outlook, dreams, goals, and intentions.
  (c) Coaching goals.
  (d) Values inventory.

- Monitoring coaching goals

  (a) Assessment of coaching goals.

  (b) Time frame for each phase of coaching.

Our Coaching Conversations

Using these steps as a guide, we began our coaching conversations with women micro entrepreneurs at Bangalore in December 2008. We spoke to the women initially via a videoconference, organized by Janalakshmi, our MFI partner in Bangalore. We subsequently reached them through the staff at Janalakshmi and via our many local volunteers.

Ubuntu at Work coaches *(a)* gain an understanding of the women micro entrepreneurs' life and socioeconomic context; *(b)* explore business opportunities with women micro entrepreneurs and identify action items; *(c)* find local partner non-profits that assist women micro entrepreneurs with undertaking the action; *(d)* engage designers from the Ubuntu at Work community to help the women micro entrepreneurs develop fair-trade products; *(e)* engage health care professionals in the Ubuntu at Work community to educate women micro entrepreneurs about primary health care issues; and *(f)* draw in educators from among the Ubuntu at Work community to address any education-related concerns. Online conversations are monitored and tracked by the Ubuntu at Work M&E team.

Support Database

Ubuntu at Work is developing a public database of (local/national/global) support organizations/networks that coaches can draw upon, when advising and assisting women micro entrepreneurs. This required us to identify partner non-profits and to begin developing a relationship with them. We also began developing operational maps specifying how the women micro entrepreneurs we were coaching would interact with these partner non-profits.

Our Virtual Global Office

With team members and volunteers spread across four continents and a growing number of countries our operations are inevitably conducted via the Internet and cyberspace is what we call home. We communicate virtually—our social networking platform, Facebook, emails, and videoconferencing.

Given time-zone differences, global operations can be a challenge. We have handled them efficiently and with considerable ease. Having multiple channels for communicating has been enormously helpful. Being flexible about our working hours has also been valuable. Finally, at this stage of our development, when roles and responsibilities are not rigidly allocated, our collaborative organizational structure has also helped us overcome global operational challenges.

Language differences have not been a problem either. Our various MFI and non-profit partners all communicate in English. While the women micro entrepreneurs we are coaching do not always speak English, MFI staff have helped them in translating our communications to the women and vice versa.

MEASURING OUR IMPACT

Ubuntu at Work measures its impact on three dimensions. First, have the women micro entrepreneurs we are coaching increased their income and escaped poverty? Second, have the women micro entrepreneurs gained additional skills and capabilities as a result of participating in our coaching conversations? Third, have our coaching conversations had a positive impact on the families of the women micro entrepreneurs?

Our effectiveness as an organization depends upon the accuracy and usefulness of our evaluation results. We will be partnering with Innovations for Poverty Action to help us measure our impact. Innovations for Poverty Action, a non-profit based in New Haven, Connecticut, relies primarily on randomized controlled trials (RCTs) to achieve highest quality results—comparable to the evaluations used by the medical profession.

The standard technique for measuring program impact used by most MFIs and non-profits involves comparing the outcomes of participants to the outcomes of a similar group of non-participants. But such an analysis does not produce a reliable estimate of a program's impact, because it compares people who "chose" to participate to people who did not. Such comparisons do not account for the subtle differences, intrinsic and/or extrinsic, between people who receive a service and people who do not.

Randomized controlled trials are one of the best ways to isolate the impacts of a specific program from other factors, such as other programs offered in the region, general macroeconomic growth, a short-term event, or even a personal quality that might make one individual more successful than another. By identifying a group of participants and separating them randomly into otherwise similar control and treatment groups, randomized trials will allow us to reliably conclude whether a particular program is responsible for generating positive changes in income, health, education, or other poverty-related areas.

Our impact evaluation technique also allows us to study the extent to which the impact of our coaching conversations is replicable. Our operational model of coaching women micro entrepreneurs in a variety of countries, engaged in a range of business activities and based in both urban and rural contexts, allows us to measure our scalability. An evaluation of our impact will indicate (a) whether an idea worked in a particular place and time with a particular group of people and (b) whether the same results hold in different contexts.

WHERE WE ARE

Our coaching conversations are beginning to have impact. Ubuntu at Work is currently helping over 100 women micro entrepreneurs in India, and is reaching out to another 50 women micro entrepreneurs in Egypt. Our initiative in India has helped women micro entrepreneurs in the Ubuntu at Work community produce eco-friendly jewelry and embroidered bags. Our local volunteers and staff have helped train the women, share ideas about professionalism, branding, quality control, etc., with the women. Today, our women are producing products with support from volunteers, but increasingly, it is clear they have gained the capabilities to do so independently.

Ubuntu at Work is developing Ubuntu at Work chapters around the world to help sell the products our women micro entrepreneurs are producing. By the end of 2009 we expect to have functioning local chapters in New York City, Washington. D.C., Seattle, San Francisco, London, Dublin, Dubai, and New Delhi. Members of these local chapters will play a critical role in marketing Ubuntu at Work products, and in brainstorming about future products.

MY VISION FOR UBUNTU AT WORK

I believe Ubuntu at Work will become a one-stop portal for all things connected to assisting women micro entrepreneurship. I hope MFIs in different countries reach us and connect their female clients to our coaches and thus help them identify how they could use their microfinance strategically and earn more. I believe designers and artists will connect to Ubuntu at Work and design products collaboratively with women micro entrepreneurs using our social networking platform.

Ubuntu at Work expects to have coaching relationships with 12,000 women micro entrepreneurs in India, Egypt, and possibly South Africa and Botswana by the end of our third year. We expect to help these women micro entrepreneurs enhance their capabilities. Specifically, we expect to help these women develop entrepreneurial business strategies, implement these plans, and increase their revenues and assets.

We anticipate that the coaching conversations will have a positive impact on women's families as well. We involve educators and public health professionals in the coaching conversations to help, as needed, women micro entrepreneurs respond better to the education needs of their children and address their public health concerns.

We encourage the women micro entrepreneurs who have been helped by our coaching to reach out and assist other women in their community trapped in poverty. Where member women micro entrepreneurs decide to produce goods, Ubuntu at Work coaches explore whether they can partner with other women micro entrepreneurs in the communities and thus enhance their capabilities. And where women micro entrepreneurs need supplemental microfinance to implement their business plans, Ubuntu at Work will raise micro loans from within the community and outside sources for them.

As a result we expect the societies of our member women micro entrepreneurs to be transformed with many other survivalist micro enterprises becoming entrepreneurial. The success of some women is likely to inspire thousands of other women to explore entrepreneurial business strategies as well. We hope this will lead these other women micro entrepreneurs to reach out to our non-profit partners, MFIs, and to Ubuntu at Work staff and coaches.

We also expect Ubuntu at Work to become the online portal for MFIs and non-profits assisting women micro entrepreneurs. We anticipate that they will turn to Ubuntu at Work to access resources in our public database to assist women. They are also likely to draw on the skills and experience of our coaches for their own activities.

Finally, Ubuntu at Work is likely to transform how people in developed countries perceive and relate to women micro entrepreneurs in developing countries and vice versa. Social networking tools are increasingly indispensable for making sustainable development for all a reality.

CHAPTER 7

Social Entrepreneurship in a Traditionally Profit-centered Industry

Steven F. Young

I'd like to share the story of how one company went from zero to a billion dollars in assets and along the way created a unique brand that has captured worldwide attention as one of the most socially progressive companies within its industry. I'll also mention the benefits and successes this company has experienced due to its social initiatives and hopefully, you'll find some of them relevant and applicable to your own company.

THE WAINWRIGHT STORY

Wainwright Bank has always contemplated two bottom lines. The social justice platform, our second bottom line, is in fact fueled by the business platform—they are mutually supportive and the success of one depends on the other. Since its founding the bank has become an entrepreneurial success story, as well as a catalyst for social change. This is predominately due to the vision and beliefs of the bank's co-founder and co-chairman, Bob Glassman. Allow me to provide a little context.

Bob is referred to as a social activist disguised as a banker. His experiences in the 1960s as a platoon leader in Vietnam and later as a war protester while attending Harvard Business School exposed him to the social inequities of our society. Later, upon attaining financial success, he became a philanthropist with a focus on civil liberties and social justice. All this occurred prior to the founding of the bank and is the source from which Wainwright's socially progressive agenda is derived.

Bob has been recognized for his achievements innumerable times including receiving the *Boston Business Journal's* first annual CEO Social Leadership Award, the Civil Rights Corporate Leadership Award from the Lawyers' Committee for Civil Rights of the Boston Bar Association, and last year received Banker of the Year Award from *American Banker*, one of the most prestigious honors within the industry.

So imagine this: it's 1985 and the publicly traded company you started 10 years ago is being taken over in a hostile bid by outside investors, but by some chance turn in the market you end up making millions for yourself and your investors. Your investors are, of course, quite impressed with your business savvy, and now want to know what you'll do for them next.

If you were John Plukas and Bob Glassman, the co-founders and current co-chairmen of Wainwright Bank, you'd, well, start a bank!

Wainwright Bank & Trust Company was founded in 1987 as a publicly traded private bank for wealthy individuals and institutions, based upon a European boutique-banking model. The name "Wainwright" is derived from H.C. Wainwright & Company, a now defunct brokerage house originally founded in the early 19th century that had catered to the blue-blood Brahmins of Boston. For a short time John and Bob ran a mutual fund for H.C. Wainwright and when they started Wainwright Bank, they received permission to use the name to lure some of the brokerage's clients to their new enterprise.

In the economic downturn of the late 1980s and early 1990s nearly every bank in the country was experiencing difficulties. Many failed. John and Bob took a hard look at their fledgling bank and decided that expanding the customer base to include the average consumer was a smart move in those uncertain times. So in 1992 Wainwright Bank purchased three former branches of the then recently failed Coolidge Bank and threw its hat into the retail banking arena.

That's where I come in. After having worked in retail for 13 years at Shawmut Bank, John and Bob hired me in 1992 to create and manage their new Retail division. It was an interesting job interview. They stated they wanted to influence the banking industry by creating a new model and definition of success, and to profitably allocate capital to underserved markets. Bob said, "we'd like to contemplate a second bottom line, a noble social experiment if you will." At the time I wasn't quite sure what that meant, but was instinctively drawn to such a progressive concept.

So I gathered the employees of the three new branches and explained we had a once in a lifetime opportunity here—to create the ideal bank—and have fun doing it. They were like, "huh?"

We made long lists of all the things we loved and hated at the banks we had previously worked for, and what our customers had loved and hated. From that we created a strategic plan that still guides us to this day. Basically, our three-part strategy is to provide true financial value, an outstanding customer experience, and a commitment to social justice. Wainwright's tagline, "Banking on Values," reflects this strategy.

In 1992, none of us, including Bob, really knew what tangible form this social commitment would take. I've been asked many times what the strategic plan for implementing our so-called social agenda was; you know, what our three-year and five-year plan were. But there was none. Our social agenda has developed organically over time—we do what we sense is the right thing to do. Choosing to take the high road, if you will, even if it means stretching outside our comfort zone sometimes, or mustering some institutional courage, that's the coin of the realm within the corporate social responsibility movement—legitimacy, transparency, and consistency.

Today, Wainwright is a state chartered commercial bank headquartered in Boston with 12 branches throughout Greater Boston. President and CEO, Jan Miller joined the bank in 1993 and, along with John and Bob, have guided the bank through strong and steady growth. Of the 8,500 banks currently existing in the United States, Wainwright is now among the 600 largest with $1 billion in assets. In addition to the Private Banking department, which traces its roots to the founding of the bank, and the retail branch network, the bank has thriving consumer and commercial lending areas and a wholly owned investment subsidiary, Heritage Capital Management.

While we are publicly traded, John and Bob own the majority of the voting stock so the bank cannot be taken over by outside shareholders; they have consistently stated the bank will remain independent, thus providing stability for both customers and employees.

We basically offer the same products and services, at the same pricing, within the same market as our competitors. But as we've been told several times by bank analysts, consultants, and other industry observers, Wainwright is unlike any other bank in the country, even those that profess to be socially responsible.

Now might be a good time to do the obligatory reading of our mission statement:

> With a sense of inclusion and diversity that extends from the boardroom to the mailroom, Wainwright Bank & Trust Company resolves to be a leading socially progressive bank, committed equally to all its stakeholders—employees, customers, communities and shareholders alike.

As dry as that sounds, at its heart our mission statement reflects the concepts of collaboration and partnership. All our stakeholders have an equal seat at the table. In the typical corporate model, shareholder concerns reign supreme, and in most cases it still is the only consideration. We think this is a very one-dimensional view and one that will be increasingly not sustainable as society continues to move toward greater social and global consciousness.

THE SOCIAL AGENDA

When I describe our social agenda, I like to break it down into internal and external practices. This is where the social justice rubber meets the road, so to speak.

Internal Practices

Internally we have management practices that have been lauded nationally as among the most progressive. We encourage diversity throughout the bank. Our board of directors consists of nine outside members of which two are female and two are African-American. Of our 67 officers, 37 percent are female and 12 percent are minorities. Among all 166 employees, a third of them speak 22 languages other than English, from Arabic to Ukrainian, and 10 percent are openly gay or lesbian, including two senior vice presidents.

We believe that by creating an open and embracing environment, employees can bring their whole selves to work each day. The rewards are great: loyalty, retention, increased productivity, and public recognition such as being named one of the Best Places to Work in Massachusetts, or along with AT&T, Subaru, and Starbucks, being ranked among the Top 10 companies in the country for gay and lesbian employees.

Wainwright was one of the first companies to endorse the National Organization for Women's "Workplace Pledge," which among other things, allows employees to organize if they wish (although considering the incredible benefits Wainwright employees receive I can't imagine that happening). The bank provides a minimum "living wage" to all full-time employees that, according to the non-profit group United for a Fair Economy, is currently $11.27 an hour.

Back in the mid-1990s the bank lobbied the Massachusetts Bankers Group Insurance Plan, for 2 years, to obtain employee domestic partner benefits for same-sex couples. We eventually received a letter stating they had decided to not only make these benefits available to Wainwright Bank, but to all 160-member banks and their 10,000 employees, primarily due to our efforts. Wainwright became the first bank in the state to offer this coverage.

Within the banking industry, a teller trainee is generally provided a one week paid vacation annually; at Wainwright every full-time employee receives a minimum of three weeks paid vacation.

We provide flex-time schedules and job sharing. Employees receive a generous benefit package including full dental coverage, free life insurance, a health club subsidy, and a 401(k) plan that is nearly unmatched in the industry.

An employee's vacation, sick days, and personal days are combined into a pool, available for use for any reason, whether personal illness, caring for a sick child, or a mental health day at the beach—there's no need to call in pretending to be sick. This recognizes our employees have lives and obligations outside the bank, provides them with dignity and respect, and we believe, increases loyalty, retention, and productivity.

Our employees receive a subsidy to encourage public transportation usage to help reduce congestion and pollution. And once a month for the last decade we have held "Casual for a Cause Fridays" where employees pay a fee to dress casual; the total amount raised is matched by the bank and donated to a non-profit nominated by employees.

The tangible benefits to all this? Again, greater productivity: the average community bank of our asset size generally has 20 percent more employees—as I'm quite sure you're aware, employee compensation is usually the greatest expense for any company.

Dedicated employees: employee turnover is expensive. When we held our most recent off-site strategic planning session, the facilitator marveled that in the eight years he had been meeting with us, only one of the 20 officers in attendance was new. In addition, we often receive resumes from people who assert they are not generally looking for a new job, but if something should become available at Wainwright, they'd love to join us.

Customer loyalty: I believe one primary key to customer loyalty—and greater profitability—is this: if employees are happy, customers will be happy too. It's a simple concept and one that many of our competitors don't seem to get!

External practices

In addition to our internal practices, our external practices include community development lending, offering unique products, getting involved in environmental initiatives, contributing to philanthropy strategically, and being an advocate on social issues.

Community Development Lending

Partnerships and collaboration are at the heart of our external activities. This includes our lending practices, how we invest our depositors' money, the products and services we offer, our philanthropy, and seemingly unique to Wainwright, our social advocacy.

Wainwright is one of the few banks in the country with a department solely committed to socially responsible community development lending. Back in the early 1990s the founding executive manager of this group, and now all five of her current lenders, employed unique insight and techniques to successfully underwrite highly complex loan packages for non-profit borrowers. To date the bank has provided over $700 million of these loan commitments to finance projects such as homeless shelters, food banks, affordable and special-needs housing, HIV/AIDS services, immigrant services, inner-city schools, community health centers, and breast cancer research, among other progressive causes.

Our clients consist of a who's who roster of non-profits in the Greater Boston area including: the Pine Street Inn, Rosie's Place, the Massachusetts Breast Cancer Coalition, The Trust for Public Land, AIDS Action Committee, Greater Boston Food Bank, Union of Concerned Scientists, New England Foundation for the Arts, Oxfam America, The Boston Foundation, Earthwatch, Amnesty International, and many others. For the Pine Street Inn alone we've financed over $15 million dollars in loans for a dozen projects over the last 18 years.

Community development lending is a significant part of our business strategy. Currently, over 50 percent of our commercial loan portfolio is committed to these types of loans. The vast majority of commercial banks in this country couldn't say even 1 percent of their portfolio—if any—was allocated to this sector.

Bankers generally assume these loans are unprofitable and risky, and just another form of charity. But nothing could be further from the truth. Our community development loans are not discounted—they are market priced just like any commercial loan we book, so they are quite profitable. But here's the amazing part: of the $700 million in these types of loans we've provided, we've never lost a penny. Hardly any bank in the country could point to a loan portfolio segment of $700 million and say they had never experienced a loss.

The question arises, if this is such good business, why don't more banks do it? Beyond ignorance of the historic performance of these loans, most banks do not have the underwriting know-how and do not want to commit the resources necessary to do it. Our Community Development Lenders are personally motivated to make these loans and often get involved far beyond the role of a typical banker. They've helped non-profits establish functional board of directors. They've also coordinated—and at times, mediated between—the needs and desires of various constituencies such as grassroots community groups, government agencies, and charitable foundations in order to see a project realized.

So beyond the financial, what are the other tangible benefits of socially responsible community development lending?

New business: over the years Wainwright has developed a reputation as the bank that seeks opportunities to help non-profits realize their objectives. In many cases they come to us first if they are looking for project financing. That's a Madison Avenue dream—to have first right of refusal to new business. Nearly all the non-profits we provide loans to move their deposit accounts to us as well; some of them are quite substantial. And we have the opportunity to interact with the boards, employees, and volunteers of these organizations, many of whom switch their personal banking relationships to Wainwright.

Customer acquisition and loyalty: our customers are aware that their deposits—be it their paycheck, savings account, or retirement Certificate of Deposit (CD)—help fund these loans. We attract many new customers because they like the idea their money is supporting social change. And once with us, they not only become fiercely loyal, but also are motivated to tell their family and friends about us.

Public relations: not only has there been extensive media coverage about the projects we've financed, the bank has received numerous awards, including the US Treasury's "Bank Enterprise Award" multiple times over the last nine years. The award recognizes a bank's commitment to providing financing for projects located in underserved communities and is accompanied by a cash reward. Over the last nine years Wainwright has received over $1.8 million dollars from this program—the money can be allocated any way we wish.

Unique Products

In addition to our community development lending, Wainwright has created some unique products within the banking industry.

In 2001 we launched an online service for non-profits called CommunityRoom.net that, among other things, offers free hosted web pages to any non-profit client, and the ability to accept online donations. Using a simple content management program similar to MS Word, non-profits create their own pages in which they can describe their mission and programs, seek volunteers, upload graphics, post their events, and link to their own websites.

Visitors to the site can review a non-profit's programs and services, make a donation, read tips on how to be a strategic donor, or access a library of position papers on social topics such as HIV/AIDS, the current state of civil liberties, and global sustainability. Donors also have the option of becoming members so each time they visit the site, they don't have to re-enter their personal information and at tax time can print out a history of their giving.

Over 200 of the bank's 500-plus non-profit clients have joined CommunityRoom.net and donations generated through this channel totaled $1.1 million last year. Industry observers tell us no other bank in the world offers such a product.

Other examples of collaboration and partnership are The Wainwright Bank Green Loan and the Equal Exchange CD.

In 1999 Solar Boston and the Massachusetts Consumers Energy Alliance approached us and asked if we would consider offering a discounted home equity loan for homeowners to finance the installation of solar energy systems. We thought it was a great idea and have since expanded The Green Loan to include financing for a wide variety of energy-efficient home improvements.

Last year we collaborated with one of our clients, Equal Exchange—a Fair Trade coffee, tea, and chocolate merchant—to create what we are told is the first of its kind product in the banking industry. The Wainwright Bank Equal Exchange CD is a three-year certificate of deposit that provides a competitive interest rate for depositors and also acts as collateral for a line of credit to Equal Exchange. As the CD deposits grow, so does the available credit to Equal Exchange, which in turn enables them to further provide third world farmers with a livable income.

Environmental Initiatives

One area the bank has received significant and continuing attention for is our environmental initiatives.

Every company seems to be going green these days, but as early as 1993, the bank began recycling waste and using recycled papers and vegetable-based inks whenever possible. Other initiatives include purchasing renewable energy and carbon offset certificates, installing low-energy lighting, purchasing Energy Star-rated computers and appliances, and building some of the first green branches in the country. The bank is recognized as a pioneer in what is now referred to as "Green Banking," including being named one of the Top 10 Green Banking Firms in the country and one of the

Top 20 Sustainable Stocks in the world. This recognition has come about at a time when the general public has become acutely aware of environmental issues, but we've been doing it for a while now.

We recently became one of the first banks in the country to offer business and non-profit clients a service we call Desktop Teller. Instead of driving to the bank to make a deposit, our clients can now scan checks to be deposited right in their offices and instantly transmit the funds over the Internet into their accounts—no need to drive to the bank.

Perhaps the most significant of our environmental activities, and one that has garnered much press attention, is building our newest branches to LEED, or Leadership in Energy and Environmental Design, specifications. The U.S. Green Building Council awards certification levels from bronze to platinum for meeting certain criteria in the design, construction, and use of sustainable building materials. Our Coolidge Corner location in Brookline became the first bank branch in New England to be certified "Silver" and our Newton Centre branch is the first one built in this country to be awarded a "Gold" certification. And both our new Harvard Square and Ashmont Station branches are awaiting LEED certification as well.

LEED criteria includes recycling at least 50 percent of demolition materials and filtering dust from the air during demolition; using recycled materials such as aluminum window frames, rubber and bamboo flooring, compressed cornhusk cabinetry, and rehabbing used furniture; installing low-energy heating, ventilating, and air conditioning (HVAC) systems, appliances and computers; maximizing the use of natural light including installing skylights and Sun Tubes; purchasing renewable energy certificates; being located next to public transportation; and other considerations.

Just as an aside, our Ashmont Station branch opening next Spring will be unusual not only because of the LEED certification, but that it will feature a full-service espresso bar in the lobby operated by Flat Black, a local Fair Trade coffee company. Considering 17,000 commuters stream daily through Ashmont Station in Dorchester, we're anticipating our joint endeavor to be mutually supportive and successful.

Strategic Philanthropy

As far as our philanthropic initiatives are concerned, we have committed to providing at least 2.5 percent of our pre-tax income annually to charitable organizations but the actual amount is generally over 3 percent, or three times the industry average. Because we have over 500 non-profit clients, we decided several years ago to provide donations exclusively to organizations we have a banking relationship with and furthermore, to favor those that focus on social justice and civil liberties issues, such as Amnesty International, Oxfam America, AIDS Action Committee, the American Civil Liberties Union, Gay & Lesbian Advocates and Defenders, and many others. We believe the organizations we partner with help define who we are and reinforce our brand.

Each year at our customer appreciation event, attended by 500 of our for-profit and non-profit clients, we present the Wainwright Bank Social Justice Award to an individual and the associated organization that has significantly contributed to social change in their particular field. The award is accompanied by a $10,000 dollar donation to the organization.

Several employees of the bank are registered to conduct financial literacy classes for public and private high school students in partnership with Project Hope. Groups of employees also volunteer their time to some of our non-profit clients such as sorting food at the Greater Boston Food Bank or serving the homeless at Pine Street Inn. The *Boston Business Journal* just this month ranked Wainwright as providing the highest number of volunteer hours per employee among 75 Boston-area companies.

In addition to CommunityRoom.net we also have physical Community Rooms at most of our branches. These are free, after-hour conference rooms available for our non-profit clients to use for meetings.

Between CommunityRoom.net, the branch Community Rooms, and our employees' volunteer efforts, our annual in-kind contribution is estimated to be the financial equivalent of $100,000 dollars.

Advocacy

Perhaps one of the most unique aspects of our corporate social responsibility, especially considering we're a publicly traded company, is our advocacy on behalf of social issues. Because of the progressive causes we champion and support in various ways, and the recognition we receive for that, we've created a certain amount of what we call "cultural capital." And as controversial as some of the issues we champion may be perceived, we're not afraid to deploy it.

For instance, one of our directors represented the bank to testify before Congress in support of the Employment Non-Discrimination Act, which would have outlawed discrimination against gays in the workplace. A few years ago our board filed a letter, and a director read it, before the Massachusetts General Court in opposition to an anti-gay constitutional marriage amendment. We were the only publicly traded company, much less a bank, to do so. We're also a signatory to several social justice initiatives including, most recently, endorsing the establishment of a living wage in Massachusetts.

Wainwright is also a major shareholder in Trillium Asset Management, the oldest and largest socially responsible investment firm in the country. Of particular interest to us is their shareholder activism, where they pool the shares held by their clients in a particular company and file proxy resolutions in order to change a negative behavior within that company. They have been quite effective at this, influencing environmental and equality practices at major corporations including MacDonald's, Johnson & Johnson, and Chrysler to name a few.

PUBLIC RELATIONS

A brand is in essence a promise to a company's stakeholders and arguably one of its most valuable attributes to be supported, protected, and nurtured. Wainwright Bank has developed into a highly distinctive brand and at this point for us *not* to use our voice in support of a particular social cause could be a reason for our stakeholders to question our commitment.

I've touched on some aspects of this previously but I'd like to just quickly mention public relations. Media coverage of Wainwright over the years has been extensive. The bank has been featured in news sources such as National Public Radio (NPR), *Time* magazine, *The New York Times*, *The Wall Street Journal*, the Today Show, CNBC, Fox News, and dozens of local, national, and international magazines and newspapers.

Just this year a book was published by Harper Collins entitled *The High-Purpose Company* by award-winning author Christine Arena. She and a group of 10 McGill University graduate students developed a new methodology to measure corporate social responsibility and then applied it to 75 companies that claim to be socially responsible. The selected companies ranged from IKEA, Toyota, GE, and Tom's of Maine to Halliburton (yes, Halliburton does claim to be socially responsible!).

When we received a galley of the book three weeks before it was published we were totally blown away to discover that Wainwright ranked number one on the list as the "ultimate high-purpose company" and was the only company mentioned in the book to have an entire chapter devoted to it.

Another award-winning and best selling author, Patricia Aburdene, who has sold 20 million copies worldwide of her *Megatrends* series of books, included a three-page description of Wainwright in her latest edition, *Megatrends 2010*. The book predicts society is now transitioning from our current "age of knowledge," which followed the industrial age, to a new age of "consciousness" wherein not just culturally creative social flakes, but blue collar workers and soccer moms will care about the ethical and sustainable behavior of the companies producing the goods and services they buy, including how their wealth is invested.

And just this month a new book was published by author Margaret Benefiel entitled *The Soul of a Leader*. In it she interviews, and I quote, "leaders who have chosen a deeper, more soulful path to building better organizations and a better society." The cover includes an endorsement by Desmond Tutu and contains extensive interviews with not only Wainwright's own Bob Glassman, but also Anita Roddick of The Body Shop, Tom and Kate Chappell, founders of Tom's of Maine, and U2 guitarist, The Edge.

As you can see, although we employ no public relations firm, we have no lack of publicity and media attention!

FINANCIAL PERFORMANCE

You've now heard how the bank provides value to our customers, employees, and communities. What about our fourth stakeholder constituency—our shareholders?

Community banks nationwide are experiencing one of the most financially challenging years in quite awhile. Shrinking margins, an inverted yield curve, and non-bank competition are working against all of us, not to mention the recent subprime mortgage meltdown and resulting credit crunch.

In the midst of all this, Wainwright continues to book loans and grow deposits, remains profitable, and continues to pay quarterly dividends. The bank has never made a subprime loan, nor do we hold any mortgage-backed securities containing subprime loans in our investment portfolio. We are not seeing the erosion in deposits that many of our peer banks are, and some of them are even experiencing negative deposit growth. And as an example of our continued growth in loans, of the 6,000 community banks in the country, *American Banker* last month ranked Wainwright fourth in home mortgage growth over the prior year at 31.8 percent.

We believe our value proposition continues to distinguish us from our competitors and not only engenders a far greater customer loyalty, but continues to attract consumers, businesses, and non-profits who are increasingly questioning how their banks are putting their money to work.

CLOSING

So thank you for paying attention to the story of, as one reporter said, "that spunky little bank from Boston" that set out to influence an entire industry and prove one can be profitable and socially conscious as well.

Wainwright is a positive proof that socially progressive banking is not an oxymoron!

REFERENCES

Aburdęne, Patricia. (2005) *Megatrends 2010: The Rise of Conscious Capitalism.* Charlottesville, VA: Hampton Roads.

Arena, Christine. (2007) *The High Purpose Company: The Truly Responsible (and Highly Profitable) Firms that are Changing Business Now.* New York, NY: Collins.

Benefiel, Margaret. (2008) *The Soul of a Leader: Finding Your Path to Success and Fulfillment.* New York, NY: Crossroad.

CHAPTER 8

Environmental Sustainability— Managing Stakeholders through Education

Vithal V. Deshpande

INTRODUCTION

In this chapter, I offer a broad overview of environmental sustainability and its various facets pertaining to public education that come from my work in the area. Environmental sustainability can broadly be defined as, "Conserving the natural resources, human surroundings and overall ecosystem without compromising human development goals" (Figure 8.1).

Because of its wide-ranging nature, environmental sustainability is included in the Millennium Development Goals (MDG) set by the United Nations (UN) and agreed upon by the participating nations to achieve by year 2015. Under UN MDG number 7, in order to achieve environmental sustainability, the following indicators are listed to represent the goals:

FIGURE 8.1 Environmental Sustainability

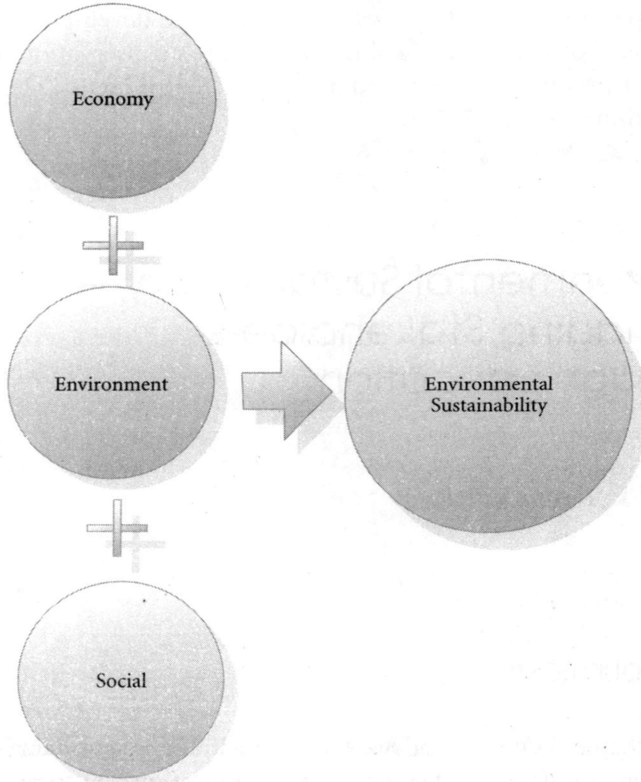

Source: Author's illustration.

- Integrate the principles of sustainable development into country policies and programs and reverse the loss of environmental resources.
- Reduce biodiversity loss, achieving, by 2010, a significant reduction in the rate of loss.
- Halve, by 2015, the proportion of the population without sustainable access to safe drinking water and basic sanitation.
- By 2020, to have achieved a significant improvement in the lives of at least 100 million slum dwellers.

Some of these targets are geared toward developing and under-developed regions of the world. However, the developed world also needs to achieve sustainability for nature's conservation, local demands, economic gains, and a healthy environment (The UN Millennium Project, 2009).

APPROACHES TO ACHIEVE ENVIRONMENTAL SUSTAINABILITY

In order to achieve the aforementioned goals, businesses and government alike are required to reduce greenhouse gas emissions responsible for climate change, reduce the environmental pollution other than that responsible for climate change, develop watersheds and provide access to clean water to the masses, develop sustainable land use patterns, and many other actions.

Historically, there are several cases of stakeholders' demands for better local conditions, especially during new development. Such development can be on a vacant parcel in the town or a new transportation project that can have significant impact on the community due to rise in vehicular traffic as well as potential of rise in property cost in the region. In case of businesses, stakeholders may demand changes in operational management or product development. For example, in the 21st century economy, with rising gas and oil prices there is a growing trend of expectations by stakeholders that businesses should be more energy efficient and potentially change or alter their product designs to suit a new energy economy.

However, there is no one "master key" to unlock the solution for environmental sustainability for all. Success of social responsibility and environmental sustainability depends on the complex interactions between government and stakeholders, or the industry and its stakeholders. This interaction requires developing strategies of interweaving economic, environmental, and social causes to deliver equity, affordability, and profitability that in turn will offer the sustainability. Therefore, it is important as decision makers to educate stakeholders and develop an informed decision-making process.

For government these are political decisions, based on the public demands and economic conditions, while, for industry these are business decisions based on market demands as well as demands from individual and institutional stakeholders.

STAKEHOLDERS EDUCATION—PATHWAYS TO ACHIEVE ENVIRONMENTAL SUSTAINABILITY

Stanford Research Institute's 1963 internal memo defined the word stakeholders as, "those groups without whose support the organization would cease to exist" (Freeman et al., 1983). The following steps can prove as guiding principles to develop approaching stakeholders through education (Figure 8.2):

FIGURE 8.2 Pathways to Stakeholders Education

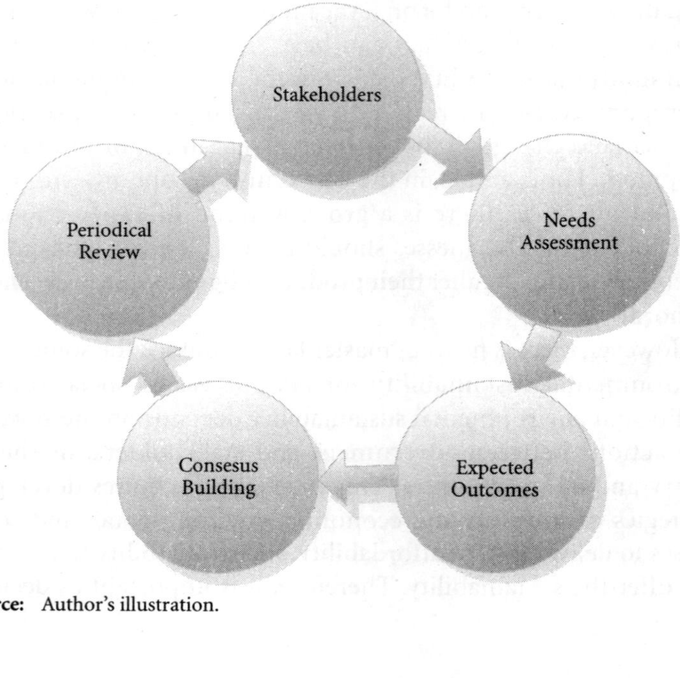

Source: Author's illustration.

- **Types of stakeholders:** As defined earlier in this section, stakeholders are typically comprised of any individual or entity that can be impacted economically, environmentally, or socially by the business operations and outcomes. Therefore for businesses, from institutional shareholders to local residents, all are stakeholders. In case of government, in addition to constituents, businesses are the stakeholders.
- **Needs assessment:** Needs assessment can be classified as regulatory needs, community needs, shareholders needs, and behavioral changes required in organization's psyche.

For example, in 1990s, recognizing arising environmental movements and demands and concerns of climate change, many companies such as Toyota changed their strategies to make greener products and sustainable operations. Similarly, with technically and financially successful recycling business model development, many states and local governments developed mandatory recycling programs to reduce rising solid waste. This effectively altered services to stakeholders and hence triggered the need to develop stakeholders' education.

- **Expected outcomes:** Expected outcomes need to be related to three primary constituents of environmental sustainability: economy, environment, and social responsibility. A framework to document such expected outcomes helps all involved and interested parties to assess the outcomes in advance. Examples of expected outcomes are related to reduction in water consumption or implementing pollution prevention technologies. In both of these cases, environmental protection, economic gains, and social responsibilities are easily achieved.
- **Consensus building:** Based on the expected outcomes, there are good chances to receive inputs from various stakeholders. Such input can typically demand more environmentally friendly operations or cost cutting without compromising any regulatory requirements. In these cases, consensus building will be valuable to engage stakeholders.

- **Periodical reviews:** Periodical reviews of completed or on-going work need to be offered. Such reviews will assist in revisiting any efforts in a constructive manner and will help to make necessary and practical changes in the system to improve continuously.

BUSINESS APPROACH

Since the beginning of 1960s to the beginning of 21st century, businesses gradually changed their perspective toward environment, initially to pollution control, then pollution prevention, environmental management system, ISO 14000 to finally evolving an all-encompassing concept of sustainability. The following subsections discuss two prominent methods to assess the environmental sustainability of corporations (Figure 8.3).

FIGURE 8.3 Stakeholders for Business Enterprise

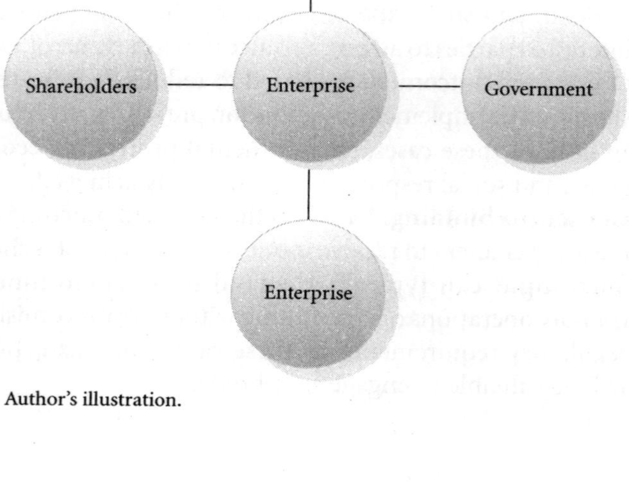

Source: Author's illustration.

DOW JONES SUSTAINABILITY INDEX

Environmental conditions, environmental movements, environmental regulations, and self-realized business profitability were the primary indicators of this period of evolution. Recognizing its importance, in 1999, Dow Jones Industrial Average initiated a new index called "Dow Jones Sustainability Index" (DJSI) to track the financial performance of the leading sustainability-driven companies worldwide (Dow Jones Sustainability Indexes, 2009).

Within the next few years of its inception, DJSI became one of the criteria for reviewing long-term prospects of the indexed corporations by institutional investors, the biggest stakeholders for the corporations. According to Dow Jones, "The quality of a company's strategy and management and its performance in dealing with opportunities and risks deriving from economic, environmental and social developments can be quantified and used to identify and select leading companies for investment purposes" (Dow Jones Sustainability Indexes, 2009). In order to find the index value, in addition to an extensive questionnaire, DJSI reviewed corporations' reports on sustainability, environment, health and safety, financial and any relevant special reporting. Today there are several hundred companies listed in various DJSI classified as World, US, Asia Pacific, Euro, and combination thereof. Companies like Allianz, Amec, Abbott, Volvo, and PepsiCo are part of DJSI. Regardless of the success of this index, information about only listed companies is certainly a limitation for the stakeholders of many other non-listed companies (Figure 8.4).

GLOBAL REPORTING INITIATIVE (GRI)

Global Reporting Initiative or simply GRI is a non-profit, multi-stakeholder network of thousands of experts in dozens of countries that review voluntary disclosure by any interested corporation for environmental sustainability in terms of social, environmental,

FIGURE 8.4 Dow Jones Sustainability Index Chart

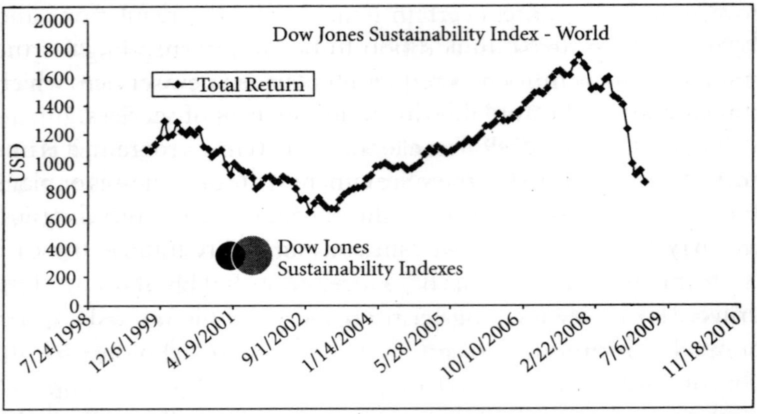

Source: http://www.sustainability-index.com

and economical performance of the company (website: www.globalreporting.org). GRI developed reporting structures for small, medium, and large organizations.

Many corporations all across the world are considering this tool as a prominent way to address stakeholders' demands to understand environmental sustainability. One peculiarity of the GRI reporting system is its ongoing efforts to develop sector-specific criteria for assessment. In this context, industry sectors such as airports, apparel and footwear, automotive, construction and real estate, electric utilities, financial services, food processing, logistics and transportation, media, mining and metals, NGO, public agency, and telecommunications are currently being developed.

GOVERNMENT APPROACH

In the case of government, the need to achieve environmental sustainability originates from its mandate—both political and societal. However, in order to serve this mandate, governments still need to struggle to find a balance. Any regulations developed at federal and state levels often create unfunded mandates. Such mandates enforce either private businesses, individuals or local and county governments to address certain issues under the regulations and to budget such items. In addition to budgetary spending for the mandates, many times new requirements need new services which may or may not be available due to uniqueness of services.

For example, to develop an electronic recycling program, it is important to make sure that there are either existing businesses or plans to encourage new start-ups who can manage electronic recycling and recovery. In absence of such businesses, such a program, in this case electronic recycling, will lack the desired sustainability. Therefore to avoid such potential problems, regulations, policies, and laws are required to have a draft reading by non-elected representatives from the society. Public hearings should be part of the process before finalization. Such careful planning to develop environmental and sustainable policies tends to have higher success rates and higher probabilities of sustained implementation.

CASE STUDIES

Rebuilding of Malden Mills Industries Inc., Lawrence, MA

Malden Mills Industries, Inc., then a privately held Lawrence, Massachusetts-based textile company, caught fire in December 1995. It was one of the biggest fins by many standards, where three connected manufacturing units were burnt down to ashes. While the company ownership on one and decisively showed its corporate responsibility to save as many jobs as possible, on the other hand, a humongous task to clean the hazardous site and rebuild. This was certainly challenging time for the business.

Stakeholders in this case were the local community, government authority, as well as the responsible team of professionals, institutional investors, and company's management. I calculated the approximate tonnage of disaster-affected debris. This debris was mixed debris of concrete, brick, steel with random impact of hazardous chemicals that spilled and burnt during the fire. In absence of any innovative approach, such debris had to be disposed of at hazardous waste landfill thus costing more money, long-term liability, and wasting a potential resource.

In this scenario, I suggested to the rebuilding team to consider reusing debris back on the site. Several questions were raised about the implications in terms of structural design of the new foundation and any other interference in the new construction. Eventually metal was separated using large magnets and the rest of the concrete and brick pieces were reused in the foundation fills for the new building. It proved to be a sustainable solution not only in its technical aspects but also for liability and cost-saving aspects which was more than $1 million in savings. This helped in consensus building resulting in further action in finding sustainable solution for the new factory building.

Cities for Climate Protection Project, City of Somerville, MA

For a local government, stakeholders are typically local residents, their elected representatives, environmental volunteers, local businesses, and the state/federal government.

In various meetings with local environmental volunteers, I identified climate change as not only a global issue but also near and dear to local dedicated environmental volunteers. It was also obvious that a well-initiated climate protection project would bring all stakeholders to the same table to act further, thus reducing greenhouse gas emissions, energy consumption, and saving tax payers' money.

After initial discussion with the chief executive officer, the mayor of the city, a decision was made to ally with the Cities for Climate Protection (CCP) program organized by the International Council for Local Environmental Initiatives (ICLEI). In order to move ahead, separate meetings with residents and elected representatives were organized. Scenarios were presented to understand the advantage of becoming a partner of the CCP program of the ICLEI. There was no cost involved but the city would be provided a summer intern to work full time to collect all data.

This project was a huge success where all stakeholders or their representative groups helped in garnering information. Reports were presented to the elected officials, mayor, senior administration, and the general public. It helped generate awareness and made a major shift in behavior, thus getting incorporated environment, energy, and sustainability in future planning. Today, Somerville has a newly constructed public school which is U.S. Green Building Council's LEED compliant. In addition to building a Green School, a Green Building Education Project was initiated with a local climate action group and Portuguese-speaking community organization. This project educated English- and Portuguese-speaking communities about how to make green choices and reduce toxicity in the building while retrofitting the existing houses and buildings. The city also changed the light bulbs, fixtures, and awarded performance-based contracts to the HVAC contractors which is going to save over $2 million, in energy and utilities.

There are local businesses that now acknowledge the importance of becoming "green." In order to satisfy the local stakeholders, predominantly residents and their patrons, a local Davis Square regional business group, initiated a project called "Go Green Davis" in collaboration with interested local residents. With this program, businesses changed their lighting systems to reduce energy consumption, started recycling program and food composting to reduce their waste and in the process reduced the impact on the environment while reducing the cost of operations.

A relatively simple program of calculating greenhouse gas emission inventory under Cities for Climate Protection Project proved to be a great educational tool that provided momentum to the government, businesses, and their stakeholders—residents and patrons in the city—to work collaboratively and to reduce consumption and achieve environmental sustainability.

CONCLUSION

In today's world, there is nothing that lives in isolation. Everything is interlinked, including sustained economy and sustainable environment. Without sustainable environmental initiatives, sustained economy is limited. A planned approach to educate stakeholders and make them a part of the team helps in making a successful solution—for environmental champions or for a focus on developing sustainable business models.

REFERENCES

Dow Jones Sustainability Indexes. (2009) "Overview." Available online at http://www.sustainability-index.com/07_htmle/indexes/overview.html (accessed on January 24, 2009).

The UN Millennium Project. "Goals, targets and indicators." Available online at http://www.unmillenniumproject.org/goals/gti.htm (accessed on January 24, 2009).

Freeman, R. Edward, Reed, David L. (1983) "Stockholders and Stakeholders: A new Perspective on Corporate Governance," *California Management Review*, 25 (3): 88–106.

CHAPTER 9

The Clean Technology Industry: Social Entrepreneurship and Sustainability

Daniel Wengrovitz and *Preeta M. Banerjee*

"Clean technology has moved from vision to reality, and it's now a priority on the CEO agenda of every company from the entrepreneurial growth companies to the multinational market leaders," said Gil Forer, Global Director of Ernst & Young's Venture Capital Advisory Group (PR Newswire, 2007). Due in part to rising energy costs and national attention to global climate change, the clean technology industry is a new and rapidly growing industry that is still being defined by consumers, financial investors, firms, and the government. Today more companies than ever have realized they can become "green," or environment-friendly, and profitable. Products and services using cleaner technology not only can reduce climate change and emissions, but also can help increase profits (Porter and Kramer, 2006).

111

However, it is getting more difficult to manage the different con-
stituent groups that give firms the "license to operate" (Thornton
et al., 2003), whereby a license to operate represents the demands of
a set of stakeholders who police and enforce compliance. Demands
include legal responsibility (the facility's regulatory permits and
statutory obligations embody the demands of regulators, legislators,
and judges), social responsibility (demands of local and national
environmental activists, local community groups, and the general
public), and economic responsibility (demands of top management,
lenders, and investors for cost-cutting and profitability). Thus, the
license model suggests that a particular firm shaped by the relative
"tightness" of its regulatory, social, and economic licenses to operate, is
enforced by external stakeholders.

On one hand are financial investors, for example, venture
capitalists pumped $7.1 billion into 922 deals in the clean technology
sector in the first quarter of 2008 alone. Clean technology now
accounts for 8.8 percent of venture capital investments (Chachere
et al., 2008). Compare this to the 1.1 percent of venture capitalist
funds in clean technology in 2000 and we notice a dramatic surge
in funding of this sector. However, with the clean technology industry, shareholders and investors have entered into investment,
unlike many others, that have the ability to "do good by doing well"
(Hamilton et al., 1993; Rivlin, 2005a, 2005b). In addition to the
capitalistic challenge of the financial bottom line, there is an
additional challenge to develop a sustainable global economy (Hart,
1997; Hart and Ahuja, 1998). Entrepreneurs in the clean technology
industry are especially susceptible to this balancing act. While
shareholders and investors play an important role in shaping this
growing sector, as populations and emerging economies further
develop, it will become increasing difficult to ignore society's
demands. Moreover, it is an industry that combines diverse intellectual areas including information technology, biotechnology, and
engineering sectors (Figure 9.1) to provide innovations that meet
the needs of stakeholders.

In this chapter, we take a look at the clean technology industry
and the intersection of sustainability and social entrepreneurship.
First, we provide a definition of clean technology and describe the

FIGURE 9.1 Positioning of Emerging Clean Technology Industry

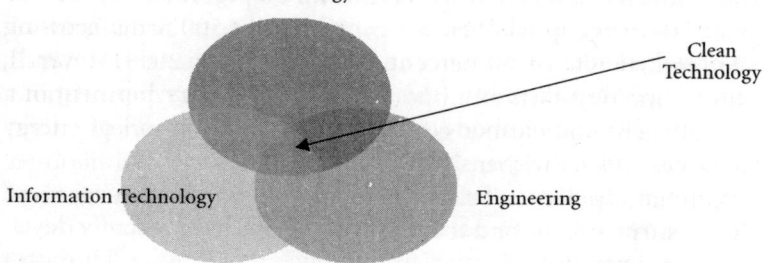

Source: Preeta Banerjee.

clean technology industry. We then proceed to look at four main stakeholder groups: government, firms, customers, and financial investors. We close with insights offered to entrepreneurs within clean technology.

WHAT IS CLEAN TECHNOLOGY?

Clean technology is a term that describes devices used to capture and distribute energy with less harmful effects on the environment than traditional techniques. The terms "alternative energy," "fuel-efficient," "renewable," and "clean" are sometimes considered substitutes. However, these terms are not interchangeable. For example, not every type of renewable energy is clean and clean is not only comprised of sustainable renewable energy practices. The World Resources Institute considers "clean power" to be energy from resources having a low impact on the health of humans, animals, and the ecosystem (Pino, 2006). These resources include: solar, wind, biomass, landfill gas, geothermal, and some types of hydropower. These resources do not emit carbon dioxide and are considered to be "clean," unlike traditional fossil fuels, which contribute to carbon dioxide emissions and global climate change. Some forms of hydropower generation may be considered renewable energy; however, it is not considered "clean" because of negative effects on the environment that influence water quality, river flows, and fish populations (Pino, 2006). In Massachusetts, where clean technology is the 10th largest sector and accounts for 10 percent of worldwide "green" venture capital, there are more than 14,500 firms, growing at an annual rate of 20 percent per year (Peter, 2008). Overall, clean technology plays an important role in the development of a more efficient and cleaner generation and distribution of energy (Guey-Lee, 2004; Swisher, 2008).

With the popularity of clean technology growing as returns grow, it is not surprising to find that many start-ups have recently developed and continue to develop technologies that require significant amounts of funding in order to grow. Overall the clean technology sector is very capital intensive mainly because of costs associated with research and development and equipment. In addition, it is much more expensive to produce the first product than it is to produce the 100,000th.

SOURCES OF SUSTAINABILITY—TYPES OF CLEAN ENERGY

Solar, wind, biomass, geothermal, and some types of hydropower are all considered to be types of renewable energy. Also referred to as "clean technology" these forms of energy have minimal effects on the environment. Traditional "dirty" forms of energy such as petroleum, natural gas, coal, and nuclear electric power all give off harmful by-products when used. Despite our knowledge of the harmful effects of these traditional forms of energy, renewable energy only accounts for about 6.6 percent of US energy consumption (Guey-Lee, 2006; Figure 9.2).

Solar

There are two types of solar devices, solar thermal cells or photovoltaic devices. Both collect sunlight and convert the sunlight into either heat or electricity. On the one hand, solar thermal devices concentrate the waves from the sun, capturing intense heat. In addition,

FIGURE 9.2 Role of Renewable Energy Consumption in the Nation's Energy Supply, 2006

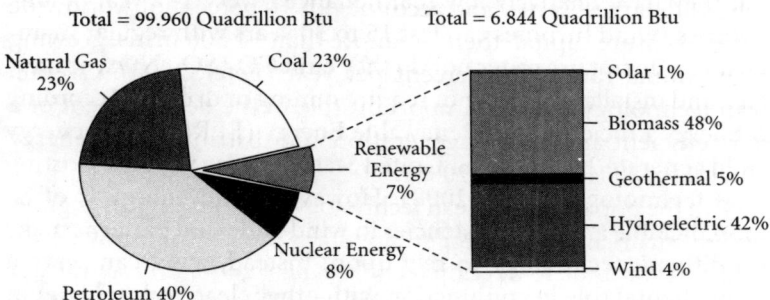

Total = 99.960 Quadrillion Btu   Total = 6.844 Quadrillion Btu

Natural Gas 23%
Coal 23%
Renewable Energy 7%
Nuclear Energy 8%
Petroleum 40%

Solar 1%
Biomass 48%
Geothermal 5%
Hydroelectric 42%
Wind 4%

Source: http://www.eia.doe.gov/cneaf/solar.renewables/page/trends/rentrends.html (accessed on May 24, 2010).

solar thermal devices can generate steam from the heat to use for electricity generation. On the other hand, solar photovoltaic devices use semiconductor materials to convert sunlight directly into electricity and then distribute this electricity throughout the grid. There are multiple types of photovoltaic devices, including c-Si, thin film, concentrating, and others such as organic, dye sensitized, micro or nano-PV. Advantages to solar energy include its abundance and potential for becoming more competitive with economies of scale. High growth rate, increasing profit margins, and multiple areas of investment are benefits of solar energy (Schyndel, 2007). Disadvantages include its expense and its limitation to harnessing power during daylight hours. More work still has to be done to create a more efficient photovoltaic cell (Laird, 2008).

Wind

Wind turbines are able to harness the power of the wind, converting wind energy into electricity. There are two categories of wind turbines, small and utility. Small wind turbines produce 300 W–100 KW, are installed at individual homes, farms, businesses, and schools, and are not on the utility grid. Utility-scale wind turbines produce 600–1,800 KW and are installed on wind farms capable of generating 10–300 MW. Some advantages of wind turbines are that they have relatively low maintenance (every 1–2 years), long lifetimes (wind turbines can last 15 to 30 years with regular maintenance), do not use water nor do they emit CO_2, SO_2, NOx, or mercury, and installation does not require mining or drilling. According to Energy Efficiency and Renewable Energy (EERE), wind energy could generate 20 percent of United States' energy with the existing wind technology (Laird, 2008). However, wind energy is often unpredictable and inconsistencies in wind and wind patterns make it a difficult technology to rely upon. Instead, wind can serve a supplemental role in conjunction with other clean technologies in providing cleaner energy (Schyndel, 2007).

Biomass

There are three subcategories of biomass: biofuels, waste, and wood-derived fuels. Biomass is considered to be a form of renewable energy because we can grow more plants and trees and we will have plenty of waste. Wood or other organic materials can be burned and the energy stored is released as heat or steam, energy that can be converted into electricity. Methane gas is released from waste, a form of energy called landfill gas that can be captured and reused. In addition, biofuels, made from biomass materials, can be combined with petroleum fuels or can be used on their own as a source of fuel. One potential pitfall for biomass is that it generates additional competition and increases demand for water and grains. Additional demands for such products increase prices of food for consumers (Schyndel, 2007).

Geothermal

Geothermal energy is captured from the interior of the earth. Wells allow steam or water to escape, powering steam turbines and electricity generators. In addition, wells can be drilled to provide heating or cooling for homes and other buildings. Geothermal power plants in California, Hawaii, Nevada, and Utah generated 14.4 billion kWh of electricity in 2004 (Guey-Lee, 2004). Geothermal energy can operate independently from centralized power plants and potentially requires less capital. However, slow development in this technology is a problem for the growth and competiveness of geothermal energy (Schyndel, 2007).

Hydropower

Moving water is a type of energy that can be converted into electricity. Forty-two percent of renewable energy is from hydropower and is only second to biomass. Hydropower plants use the flowing water (usually captured with dams) to turn a turbine which is part of a generator that turns this energy into electricity. One benefit of hydropower is its consistency, that is, the relatively constant energy supply from the fairly constant water flow (Schyndel, 2007).

THE IMPORTANCE OF CLEAN TECHNOLOGY TO THE UNITED STATES GOVERNMENT

Government demands clean innovations for similar reasons as consumers: independence from other countries, reducing climate change, and pressure from citizens and representatives (Porter and Linde, 1995). The establishment of a clean technology industry within the United States will help create additional jobs for US citizens. Jobs ranging from construction to IT to government positions will be created in order to facilitate the demand for this industry. This job creation will in turn help to fuel the US economy with a new type of technology revolution. New devices and products will help create a profitable industry that the government can subsidize. In addition, solving the energy crisis will provide the United States with new exports including new ideas and products to China, India, and other developing and developed countries to aid in their growth and need for energy independence. Lastly, the government can benefit from clean technology by becoming a leader and the first country to find solutions. This is a possible way for the United States to demonstrate its resources and power to the rest of the world in a constructive and non-violent manner. This can be considered a victory in science and technology for the United States and a way to demonstrate authority.

Another reason the government has an interest in the clean technology industry dates back to the late 19th century. The progressive era established the need for government protection of the ordinary citizen (Holcombe, 1996). The establishment of regulations is necessary for the energy industry because of the effects of traditional energies. The government steps in to regulate actions when there are negative externalities associated with these actions. Climate change affects all US citizens, not just the producers/users of energy.

Lastly, the government has a demand for clean technology due to pressure from citizens and representatives. Energy policy is a growing political issue that is on the agenda of many politicians. Citizens and representatives are becoming more aware of the harmful effects of traditional energy and our growing dependence on traditional energy. Pressure from the citizens (bottom–up approach), combined with pressure from the top–down (laws, taxes, and subsidies), make it clear that progress is necessary for clean technology products. Additionally, we are witnessing a truly global nature of the impact of policies in this arena, for example, the call for pollution reduction in order to commence with the Chinese Olympics.

Analysis of Light Technology and the Positive Effects of Government Involvement

General Electric (GE) is well known for producing the modern incandescent light bulb and with dozens of patents has been able to improve the efficiency of the incandescent light bulb since 1906 (GECIL, 1996). However, recently another type of bulb, that is, the compact florescent light bulb has become popular due to its ability to conserve more energy and last longer than the modern incandescent bulb. The modern compact fluorescent bulb uses up to 75 percent less energy and may last 10x longer than the modern incandescent bulb. However, the technology for the modern incandescent is not new, but has been around since 1976. GE shelved the design for the modern compact fluorescent bulb when it was developed in 1976 because the bulb required new manufacturing facilities that would cost $25 million. Fortunately, eventually leaked designs made it possible for other companies to copy this product and produce it (Kanellos, 2007).

There are two major problems with the integration of the fluorescent light bulb. First, the original fixed costs associated with the production of the fluorescent light bulb prevented GE from producing a cleaner technology and product. Second, there was no collaboration and co-development between firms to develop and produce this technology. Both of these problems could have been fixed with government involvement. First, the government should have helped promote this technology with subsidies or helped by directly investing in a new production facility to produce the fluorescent bulbs. Second, the government could have helped increase collaboration between firms by protecting GE's invention with stricter patents or by encouraging GE to issue licensing fees. Overall, additional support and interaction of the government with GE in the production of the modern fluorescent light bulb could have brought the more energy-efficient technology to mass markets quicker, ultimately reducing greenhouse gas emissions sooner. Looking toward the future of light technology, light-emitting diodes (LEDs) will eventually become even more efficient than the fluorescent bulb. In fact, research in LED technology has increased the efficiency of LEDs with the doubling of light output occurring about every 36 months, which is referred to as Haitz's Law (Haitz, 2006). Learning from past mistakes, the US government should help LED developers to finance additional research to bring down the costs of LED technology, in order to bring this technology to mass markets sooner. In addition, the US government should help protect the research and development of LED technology by enforcing patents and encouraging licensing and collaboration between LED development and production firms.

THE IMPORTANCE OF CLEAN TECHNOLOGY TO FIRMS

Firms are constantly monitoring the needs of consumers in order to provide "solutions." Specifically, entrepreneurial ventures have built their firms on providing a product or service that solves a problem that an average consumer may have (Shane and Venkataraman, 2000). Recently, consumers have been concerned with environmental issues like limited resource availability and climate change. Firms are able to help solve these consumer anxieties with energy-efficient technologies (e.g., appliances including refrigerators, dish washers, electronics that use less energy). The market for clean technology is growing tremendously because of its popularity among consumers, a popularity that corporations can capitalize on. There is not one "solution," but numerous solutions for each community (Figure 9.3). Clean technology products differ and may even be useless in some areas. For example, wind turbines in the open Midwest fields are much more efficient at harnessing power than a wind turbine in Washington, D.C., surrounded by buildings. In addition, corporations are ultimately run by shareholders. However, these shareholders are individuals that at the end of the day are also affected by climate change and emissions. Corporate social responsibility incorporates aspects of business with social responsibility.

The traditional view of firm success is changing from profit maximizing to a mix of profit maximizing, that is, traditional "business"

FIGURE 9.3 Stages of Product Development

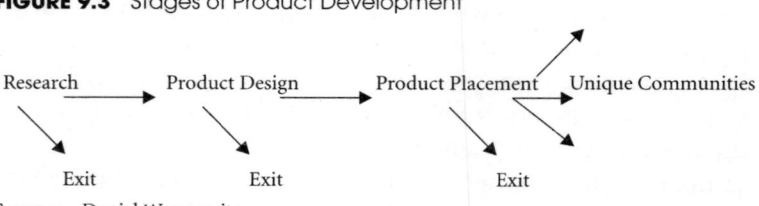

Source: Daniel Wengrovitz.

and social responsibility. Eventually this must be the way corporations view success. The purpose of a firm is not only to make a profit, but also to strive for social impact. That being said, it is also necessary for a socially responsible company to be profitable. If a socially responsible company is not profitable, it eventually shuts down and society does not continue to benefit from it. On the other hand, if a company does not concern itself with climate change, it will be left behind and be deserted by consumers. Hopefully before this occurs, government regulations and restrictions will make it unfeasible for corporations not to be concerned with climate change.

Corporate Investment in Renewable Energy: Duke Energy and Wind

Over the past few years Duke Energy, a provider of gas and electricity to Ohio, Indiana, and Kentucky, has diversified its risk and broadened its focus in energy to include renewable energies including solar and wind. In 2007, Duke Energy acquired Tierra Energy, a wind developer. A more recent purchase of Catamount Energy, for $320 million, has increased Duke Energy's wind power supply (Wang, 2008). These acquisitions illustrate forward thinking through diversification and integration of new technologies (LaMonica, 2008). According to president of Duke Energy Generation Services, Wouter van Kempen, "You can build large utility scale wind farms and power plants relatively fast compared to anything else and build them cheaper than any renewable energy at this stage. That makes wind very attractive to us." Kempen's statement illustrates not only the importance and involvement of clean technology to firms, but the importance to stakeholders as well (Duke Energy is considered a firm and a shareholder of the wind development firms). Duke Energy is one of many companies that have adopted renewable energy sources. Not only can Duke Energy be profitable, but it can be socially responsible as well, sending a strong message to shareholders, competitors, and customers of the interdependency of profitability and social responsibility.

THE IMPORTANCE OF CLEAN TECHNOLOGY
TO SHAREHOLDERS

The role of shareholders is to demand increase in shareholder value, usually measured in share price or stock price. However, shareholder value does not refer to simply monetary value, but to utility and overall satisfaction of the individual shareholder. In other words, an individual should choose to become a shareholder of corporations that will maximize the utility of the individual, not necessarily maximizing monetary returns (Porter and Kramer, 2006). For example, an investor is deciding between Company A and Company B. Predicted annual monetary returns for Company A are 8 percent and for Company B are 10 percent. However, Company A is engaged in producing clean wind turbines, while Company B harnesses energy from coal. Investor A and Investor B experience satisfaction not measured in the annual stock rate of return, and Investor C does not receive any satisfaction (Table 9.1).

TABLE 9.1 Utility Preferences of Investors

	Prefers Clean Technology?	*Company A*	*Company B*	*Preference Fulfilled?*
Annual Stock Rate of Return*		8%	10%	
Investor A (receives at least 2% satisfaction**)	Yes	√		Yes
Investor B (receives between 0 and 2% satisfaction)	Yes		√	No
Investor C (receives no satisfaction)	No		√	Yes

Source: Daniel Wengrovitz.
Notes: *Assume only monetary stock return;
**Assume satisfaction is measured such that a 1 percent increase in satisfaction = 1 percent increase in stock price.

In this model the optimal choice from the investor's perspective is for Investor A to choose Company A, while Investor B and C choose Company B. The preferences of all groups are not met.

Investor B would prefer to invest in clean technology company, but does not. Only investors that receive significant internal satisfaction from investing in clean technology products invest in the clean technology company. This model suggests a specific area where government should step in and support, specifically, to align social preferences with investment outcomes. A government subsidy in clean technology would allow companies to take in additional profit, allowing more investors like Investor B to invest in socially responsible corporations. In the Table 9.1 model, this subsidy affects Company B as well because for every dollar invested in Company A, a dollar is not invested in Company B.

THE IMPORTANCE OF CLEAN TECHNOLOGY TO CONSUMERS

There are three factors of demand from consumers: social impact, inexpensive energy, and growth. Let us begin with the social impact. A transition from traditional energy to energy harnessed from clean technology will reduce the environmental impact. Humans' everyday actions influence the environment and the ecosystem. Not only are these dirty energies altering our habitat, but these energies are running out. Goodstein (2004) believes that within this decade the world will run out of cheap, conventionally produced oil. If no further resources are discovered the world's oil supply will be exhausted by 2056 (Deming, 2003). Supply is diminished and demand is stationary, price goes up. However, there is an alternative where supply is constant or even growing. Renewable energy is potentially unlimited. We may not run out of traditional energy in our lifetime, but we do want our children's children to have the energy that we had (in fact, we want them to have cleaner, more efficient energy). We have the opportunity to provide future generations the solution of tapping an unlimited resource of energy. This idea of unlimited energy is not only attractive on a social impact level, but is also enticing on a financial level.

As renewable energy is used more and more, it will become more commonplace. Overall, the harnessing of renewable energy has become more efficient and it seems likely that the cost associated with renewable energy technology will continue to decrease in the future (Gross et al., 2003). As newer and more efficient technology is developed to capture this energy, the cost of capturing the energy will decrease (hopefully to the point where it is less expensive than traditional energy). It is not a question of if, but when renewable energy will become less expensive than traditional energy because the price of traditional energy will continue to rise, while renewable energy will continue to fall. If this pricing structure becomes reality, then regardless of social and environmental impacts the business and consumer will use renewable energy rather than traditional energy simply because it is cheaper. If business is greater than zero, then even if social impact is at the very minimum, zero, the use of renewable energy is positive. Therefore, social impact isn't even necessary (but an added benefit). This rules out intangible benefits and leaves us with pure business sense.

Finally, there is demand from consumers on the level of growth. Solving the energy crisis is not just a problem of the United States, but is a global issue and solving this dilemma may be a next step for economic growth in the United States. Solving the energy crisis will provide the United States with a competitive advantage over other countries (Porter and Stern, 2001). Other countries will want solutions which the United States can sell in the form of ideas or actual products. Similar to the arms race of the USSR and the United States, the country to discover solutions first will reap the benefits.

SMART ENERGY METERS: THE INTERSECTION OF CONSUMERS, GOVERNMENT, FIRMS, AND SHAREHOLDERS IN CLEAN TECHNOLOGY

Silver Springs, a developer of smart energy meters, is at the forefront of the clean technology movement. Smart energy meters are part of a larger smart grid solution that allows users to reduce energy consumption by 5 to 15 percent with real-time tracking and monitoring of individual residential energy usage (Ante, 2009).

State commitment, for example statewide advanced metering deployment, launched in 2006 by the California Public Utilities Commission and the California Energy Commission, have allowed for firms such as Pacific Gas & Electric to spend significant amounts on smart grid technology (Ante, 2009). In fact, Pacific Gas & Electric plans to replace all five million of its electric meters with Silver Spring's technology. Companies such as Google and Kleiner Perkins Caufield & Byers have invested in Silver Springs. These firms and their shareholders, as investors in Silver Springs, stand to be big winners if recent government support continues, such as $11 billion in the recent stimulus package to upgrade the US electric system. Government plays a major role in the development of this technology, but also has a lot to gain from supporting this technology such as more jobs for US citizens. Ultimately, start-ups such as Silver Springs incorporate all of the major players including consumers, government, firms, and shareholders in a situation where all participants can be winners in the development of smart grid clean technology.

CONCLUSION

The rise in popularity of clean technology and the increasing number of subsidies for clean technologies has made the clean technology sector more attractive, both for existing and new firms. With the introduction of clean technology comes increased pressure for firms to be more socially responsible. Firms are responders to the market and stakeholders in the sense that a corporation generates a product in reaction to the demand of a product. Stakeholders do shape development of certain technologies, although financial investors and governments are not always in line with the firms themselves, the public/consumers, and strategic corporate investors.

Growing demand for energy combined with a decreasing supply of traditional fossil fuels and increasing public awareness of climate change create a push market for clean technologies. Funders and consumers of products and services are pushing for rapid growth of clean technologies (Bradach, 2003). However, these groups along with over-ambitious and aggressive missions increase the pressure to develop clean technologies without adequate planning for growth (Austin et al., 2006; Bradach, 2003). Austin, Stevenson, and Wei-Skillern explain that opportunities for social entrepreneurs often exceed available resources. In other words, demand outweighs supply because of costs associated with new technologies. On the other hand, when we look at the supply side, expenditures lead to innovation, which helps reduce the cost of clean technologies. In turn, clean technologies help reduce climate change, and increase the demand for such technologies by generating greater public awareness of climate possibilities, and eventually greater pressure for additional clean technologies (See Figure 9.4; Lanjouw and Mody, 1996). Ultimately, new clean technology and innovation of clean technology follow demand for clean technology, pushing innovation and development.

FIGURE 9.4 Implications of One-time Expenditures in Clean Technology

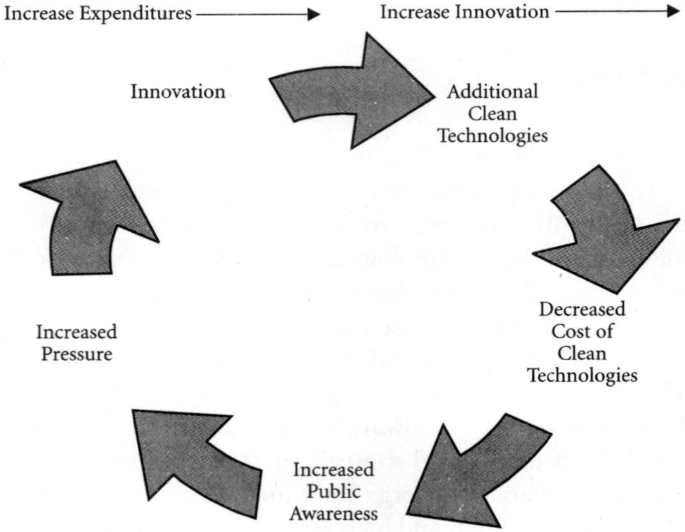

Increase Expenditures ⟶ Increase Innovation ⟶

Innovation

Additional
Clean
Technologies

Increased
Pressure

Decreased
Cost of
Clean
Technologies

Increased
Public
Awareness

Source: Daniel Wengrovitz, developed for this chapter.
Note: Increase in expenditure leads clean technology into the innovation cycle in which demand, not supply, is responsible for ongoing innovation.

CLEAN TECHNOLOGY: SOCIAL ENTREPRENEURSHIP AND SUSTAINABILITY

Sustainability and clean technology practices are of interest to the government, corporations, venture capitalists, and NGOs and citizens. The clean technology industry affects everyone. Corporations must carefully navigate through cleaner industrial practices, partnering with smaller, more innovative companies, while abiding by government regulations and public support and criticism, listening to advocates of corporate social responsibility, while still making a profit. Venture capitalists must fund innovative start-ups with fresh ideas, in a highly competitive footrace that has not yet produced any clean technology giants, while listening closely to new government regulations and subsidies. These start-ups as well as other clean technologies are funded by venture capitalists and the government (in the form of tax breaks and subsidies). NGOs and citizens watch as corporations become "green"; however, with further research many of these companies are guilty of at least one of the sins of greenwashing, that is, the sin of the hidden trade-off, the sin of no proof, the sin of vagueness, the sin of irrelevance, the sin of fibbing, or the sin of the lesser of two evils (TerraChoice Environmental Marketing, 2007). The government has to act through all of this commotion, while trying to please everyone. The actions of the government will influence the clean technology market and will ultimately put pressure on the market to develop certain types of technologies (regulations, tax breaks, and subsidies affect funding and the final product). The actions or even inaction of the government can scare or entice venture capitalists, start-ups, and corporations to particular segments of the clean technology industry.

One of the reasons many individuals support ethanol is that it uses existing infrastructure. Traditional petroleum gas stations can distribute ethanol with the same pump. In fact, ethanol is usually mixed in with petroleum (usually a 10 percent ethanol 90 percent petroleum mix). However, using existing infrastructure to produce and distribute renewable energy is not just used in ethanol distribution, but with many other types of renewable energy as well.

For example, the roofs of large department stores are terrific places to install large solar cell systems.

Corporations often have considerable power over governments and can significantly influence the economics, politics, and culture of a nation (Winston, 2002). Multinational corporations may be even less accountable for their actions because of the dependence of the hosting nation on the corporation. Nations bid over corporations, permitting them to produce in the country with the least restrictive regulations. NGOs are especially important in influencing the actions of corporations when countries and laws have interest in keeping the production in their country. However, social responsibility lies in the individual, not the corporation, and it is the duty of the corporation to serve its shareholders first (Friedman, 1970). It is the duty of the government to impose taxes and regulations in order to fund alternative projects such as environmental sustainability. However, when the government is influenced so much by the corporation that it cannot impose restrictions on the corporation, NGOs become much more important.

There are two primary strategies that NGOs use to change actions of corporations, that is, engagement and confrontation (Winston, 2002). In engagement, NGOs work with corporations to make them more socially responsible, while in confrontation, NGOs publicly name and criticize corporations that are not as socially responsible.

However, it is difficult for larger corporations to change their ways. Instead, start-ups, which are more innovative than larger corporations can lead the way in research and development for clean technology (Shan et al., 2006). Inter-firm cooperation between large and small firms can be mutually beneficial. Larger firms help support innovation in smaller firms. Smaller firms serve as a profitable addition for larger firms. Corporate social responsibility is created through the cooperation of larger corporations and new smaller firms focused on social entrepreneurship. Furthermore, NGOs form partnerships with smaller socially responsible firms, in the form of funding and leadership. Thus, a circle of relationships is formed (Figure 9.5).

FIGURE 9.5 Relationship between Corporations, NGOs, and Socially
Responsible Start-ups

Corporations   NGOs

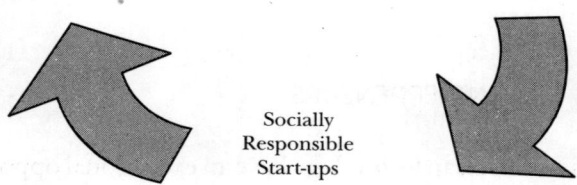

Socially
Responsible
Start-ups

Source: Daniel Wengrovitz, developed for this chapter.

In addition, corporations have begun to implement socially responsible behavior as a component of their strategy. As seen earlier, corporations such as General Electric (GE) have embraced the idea of corporate social responsibility and have placed a positive light upon themselves with their ecomagination campaign and their commitment to reduce energy use and greenhouse gas emissions. GE even has a $1 billion Cleantech Fund for investments in cleaner technology research and development. This cross-corporation business strategy has not only reduced operating costs and profitability, but has also increased consumer loyalty as well. As Porter and Kramer suggest, corporate social responsibility can be more than about cost, it can be a source of competitive advantage (Porter and Kramer, 2006). Public opinion and expectations from consumers can influence the direct sales and profitability of a firm. Firms that can incorporate new innovation and strategy will gain the respect of their competitors and consumers. Additionally, firms that ignore clean technology and energy efficiency will face public criticism and consumer dissatisfaction (e.g., Walmart and Nike). Therefore,

corporations' willingness to assist in development of clean technology and energy-efficient practices should be included in a firm's
strategy and overall profitability. Reputation is a summation of the
past actions of a firm as well as proceedings that the firm must carry
in the future. In addition, as Warren Buffet has eloquently said, "It
takes twenty years to build a reputation and five minutes to destroy
it" (Gaultier-Gaillard and Louisot, 2006). Firms engage in corporate
social responsibility within their existing business strategy, not as
a separate fragmented component of charity or philanthropic work.

LESSONS FOR ENTREPRENEURS

Entrepreneurs in clean technology have an exceptional opportunity
to launch companies that are both highly profitable and socially
responsible, that is, meet the demands of stakeholders. In the near
future, the $6 trillion energy industry could potentially transform
into a much larger clean technology industry. More efficient, renewable, and cleaner solutions remain untapped, waiting research and
development from the next great entrepreneur. Currently, it seems
that most individuals have a preference for cleaner technology.
For clean technologies that are already within reach of the price of
existing technologies, further innovation will lead to further cost
reductions and a more efficient product. It is very possible that
these clean technologies will not only benefit society, but also may
become cheaper than existing energy solutions. Clean technology
products that are significantly cheaper than existing energy solutions
are the greatest opportunity for entrepreneurs because regardless
of individual preferences the end user will purchase this product
because it is cheaper.

REFERENCES

Ante, Spencer E. (2009) "Silver Spring: A Growing Presence in Green Tech," *Business
Week*, February 18, 2009.

Austin, J., Stevenson, H., and Wei-Skillern, J. (2006) "Social and Commercial Entrepreneurship: Same, Different, or Both?" *Entrepreneurship Theory and Practice*, 30(1): 1–22.

Bradach, J. (2003) "Going to Scale: The Challenge of Replicating Social Programs," *Stanford Social Innovation Review*, 1(1): 19–25.

Chachere, C., Peterson, L., and Mendell, E. (2008) "Venture Capital Investment Declines in Q1 2008 According to the Moneytree Report," *National Venture Capital Association*, 21: 1–4.

Deming, D. (2003) "Are We Running Out of Oil?" National Center for Policy Analysis Background Paper No. 159.

Friedman, Milton. (1970) "The Social Responsibility of Business is to Increase its Profits," *The New York Times*, September 13, 1970.

Gaultier-Gaillard, Sophie and Louisot, Jean-Paul. (2006) "Risks to Reputation: A Global Approach," the Geneva Papers, 31(3), July, pp. 425–45(21). Basingtoke: Palgrave Macmillan.

General Electric Consumer and Industrial Lighting (GECIL). (1996) "TUNGSRAM: A Short History." Available online at http://www.tungsram.hu/tungsram/downloads/tungsram/tu_short_history_1896-1996.pdf (accessed on April 12, 2010).

Goodstein, D. (2004) "Out of Gas," American Geophysical Union, San Francisco, CA.

Gross, R., Leach, M., and Bauen, A. (2003) "Progress in Renewable Energy," *Environment International*, 29(1): 105–22.

Guey-Lee, Louise. (2004) "Renewable Energy Trends 2004 Edition," *Renewable and Alternative Fuels Energy Information Administration*, 2004 edition. Available online at http://www.eia.doe.gov/cneaf/solar.renewables/page/trends/rentrends04.html (accessed on April 12, 2010).

Guey-Lee, Louise. (2006) "Renewable Energy Trends 2006 Edition," *Renewable and Alternative Fuels Energy Information Administration*, 2006 edition. Available online at http://www.eia.doe.gov/cneaf/solar.renewables/page/trends/trends.pdf (accessed on April 12, 2010).

Hamilton, S., Hoje, J., and Statman, M. (1993) "Doing Well While Doing Good? The Investment Performance of Socially Responsible Mutual Funds," *Financial Analysts Journal*, 49(6): 62–66.

Hart, S. (1997) "Beyond Greening: Strategies for a Sustainable World," *Harvard Business Review*, 75(1): 66–76.

Hart, S., and Ahuja, G. (1998) "Does it Pay to be Green? An Empirical Examination of the Relationship between Emission Reduction and Firm Performance," *Business Strategy and the Environment*, 5(1): 30–37.

Holcombe, R. (1996) "The Growth of the Federal Government in the 1920s," *The Cato Journal*, 16(2): 1–22.

Kanellos, Michael. (2007) "Father of the Compact Fluorescent Bulb Looks Back," CNET News, August 16, 2007.

Laird, Daniel L. (2008) "Renewable Energy Overview," Clean Technology & Sustainable Industries Conference & Trade Show, Hynes Convention Center, Boston, MA, June 1, 2008.

LaMonica, Martin. (2008) "Corporate Giants Push Into Clean-Tech Venture Investing." CNET News, August 4, 2008, Green Tech ed.

Lanjouw, J., and Mody, A. (1996) "Innovation and the International Diffusion of Environmentally Responsive Technology," *Research Policy*, 25(4): 549–71.

Peter, T. (2008) "States Vie to Attract Clean-Tech Industries," *The Christian Science Monitor*, 11. Available online at http://www.csmonitor.com/USA/2008/0411/p03s05-usgn.html (accessed on April 12, 2010).

Pino, S. (2006) "Switching to Green: A Renewable Energy Guide for Office and Retail Companies," World Resources Institute, pp. 1–26. Available online at http://www.wri.org/publication/switching-to-green (accessed on April 12, 2010).

Porter, M., and Kramer, M. (2006) "Strategy & Society: The Link between Competitive Advantage and Corporate Social Responsibility," *Harvard Business Review*, 84(12): 78–92.

Porter, M., and van der Linde, C. (1995) "Green and Competitive: Ending the Stalemate," *Harvard Business Review*, 73(5): 120–34.

Porter, M., and Stern, S. (2001) "Innovation: Location Matters," *Sloan Management Review*, 42(4): 28–36.

PR Newswire. (2007) "Global Venture Capital Investments in Clean Technology Surge," September 27, 2007. Available online at http://www.encyclopedia.com/doc/1G1-169103938.html (accessed on April 12, 2010).

Rivlin, G. (2005a) "Green Investments: The Color of Money," *International Herald Tribune*, 23(1): 1–2.

Rivlin, G. (2005b) "Green Tinge is Attracting Seed Money to Ventures," *The New York Times*, 22(1): 1–2.

Schyndel, Zoe Van. (2007) "Clean or Green Technology Investing," Investopedia. Available online at http://www.investopedia.com/articles/07/clean_technology.asp (accessed on April 12, 2010).

Shan, Weijan, Walker, Gordon and Kogut and Bruce. (2006) "Interfirm Cooperation and Startup Innovation in the Biotechnology Industry," *Strategic Management Journal*, 15(5): 387–94.

Shane, S., and Venkataraman, S. (2000) "The Promise of Entrepreneurship as a Field of Research," *Academy of Management Review*, 25(1): 217–24.

Swisher, R. (2008) "Wind Power Outlook 2008," *Wind: Powering a Cleaner, Stronger America*. Washington, DC: American Wind Energy Association.

TerraChoice Environmental Marketing. (November 2007) "The 'Six Sins of Greenwashing'," A "Green Paper" by TerraChoice Environmental Marketing Inc. Available online at http:/www.terrachoice.com/6 files_sins.pdf (accessed on February 21, 2009).

Thornton, D., Kagan, R., and Gunningham, N. (2003) "Sources of Corporate Environmental Performance," *California Management Review*, 46(1): 127–41.

Wang, Ucilia. (2008) "Duke Energy Buys More Wind Power," Greentechmedia, June 26, 2008.

Winston, Morton. (2002) "NGO Strategies for Promoting Corporate Social Responsibility," *Ethics & International Affairs*, 16(1): 71–87.

Greening the Built Environment

Ameeta Soni

Making a business more sustainable helps the planet in many ways, while contributing to the bottom line. There has been a lot of interest in the last few years in designing green buildings. However, existing buildings account for the largest percentage of building energy consumption and environmental impact. Forty percent of global emissions are attributed to buildings. Increasingly, organizations are looking for ways to make their buildings more sustainable, reduce their environmental impact, and promote a healthier built environment.

In addition to extending building life and providing cost savings, sustainable building practices also enhance employee productivity, as a healthier workplace leads to healthier employees, translating to less absenteeism, greater retention, and improved recruiting.

In this chapter, readers will learn approaches for evaluating sustainability opportunities, strategies to measure cost savings, and how to focus their financial and human resources for the greatest impact. The case study will profile the green initiatives an organization implemented for its existing buildings, highlighting the approach taken, metrics used, and the expected benefits, including the return on investment (ROI).

When it comes to energy consumption and greenhouse gases, one does not have to look hard to find the bad news. The building and construction sector is a major contributor to global warming, accounting for (UNEP Sustainable Building and Construction Initiative 2006):

- 25–40 percent of global energy consumption
- 30–40 percent of solid waste generation
- 30–40 percent of global greenhouse gas emissions

The good news can be harder to come by. But every challenge presents opportunities, and as an individual, a real estate owner or manager, or a member of the building industry, one can be a part of a movement to reduce energy consumption and promote sustainability.

DEFINING SUSTAINABILITY TODAY

Sustainability is defined by the World Commission on Environment and Development as "meeting the needs of today without compromising the ability of future generations to meet their own needs." While there is still no single standard for sustainable building, the Leadership in Energy and Environment Design (LEED) standards for both new construction and existing buildings are emerging as recognized benchmarks for high-performance green buildings. A green building uses less energy, water, and natural resources, creates less waste and is healthier for the people living inside compared to a standard building.

Developed by the U.S. Green Building Council (USGBC), the building industry coalition formed in 1993 to promote sustainability of the built environment, the LEED Green Building Rating System provides building owners and operators with standards to reference in promoting the sustainability of their facilities. LEED's rating system provides for four certification levels—Certified, Silver, Gold, and Platinum. These levels are awarded based on the number of credits a building receives for satisfying specific performance benchmarks within various categories of sustainability, such as energy efficiency, water conservation, and indoor air quality.

Until fairly recently, green buildings were most often discussed in the context of new construction. The USGBC initially targeted its energy and environmental rating system at new buildings. This standard, known as Leadership in Energy and Environmental Design for New Construction or LEED-NC, defines six categories in which credit points are awarded toward certification: sustainable sites, energy and atmosphere, water efficiency, indoor environmental quality, materials and resources, and innovation in design.

New construction techniques and technologies still garner the lion's share of the spotlight when it comes to media coverage related to building sustainability. But it is the facilities that already exist that represent the vast majority of building energy consumption and environmental impact. According to the USGBC, in the United States, existing buildings account for 36 percent of total energy use and 65 percent of electricity consumption. They make up 30 percent of greenhouse gas emissions and 30 percent of waste output, a total of 136 million tons annually.

In recognition of this fact, the LEED-NC standards eventually led to the development of a similar rating system for existing buildings (LEED-EB), which was released in 2004. This standard adds one additional category to the LEED-NC performance criteria, related to building operation and upgrades.

SUSTAINABILITY IN INDIA

In India, the majority of the LEED rating system points are applicable in a context specific to Indian challenges. LEED INDIA is applicable to both new and existing buildings and addresses the national priorities: water, overburden of urban infrastructure, energy, waste disposal, and resource utilization (materials). There is higher weight assigned to water efficiency, for example, potable water reduction and using gray water for landscape irrigation and air conditioning make-up.

Promotion of energy efficiency in the building sector is very important in India because of the constraints on energy supply. The Indian Energy Conservation Act 2001 encourages energy-efficient design or retrofit of buildings for commercial buildings that have a connected load of 500 kW or greater and buildings with conditioned floor area in excess of 1,000 m². It is currently a voluntary scheme but could be made mandatory within the next few years, potentially yielding an annual savings of 1.7 billion units of power. The Building Energy Code, ECBC 2007, developed by the Indian Bureau of Energy Efficiency, is mandatory for commercial buildings and building complexes that have a connected load of more than 500 kW or a contract demand of 600 kVA or greater. The Indian Bureau of Energy Efficiency (BEE) has launched several initiatives to encourage the retrofit of existing public buildings in order to reduce their operating energy consumption.

The Energy Research Institute (TERI) has developed a tool for measuring and rating a building's environmental performance in the context of India's varied climate and building practices. This tool, Green Rating for Integrated Habitat Assessment (GRIHA), uses its qualitative and quantitative assessment criteria to "rate" a building on the degree of its "greenness." The rating can be applied to new and existing building stock of varied functions, including commercial, institutional, and residential buildings, but is currently used primarily for new construction. The rating system aims to achieve efficient resource utilization, enhanced resource efficiency, and better quality of life in the buildings.

The GRIHA rating system is a voluntary scheme. It has incorporated the voluntary building codes/guidelines being developed by the Bureau of Energy Efficiency, the Ministry of Non-Conventional Energy Sources, the Ministry of Environment and Forests, and the Bureau of Indian Standards.

A building is assessed based on its predicted performance over its entire life cycle—inception through operation. At the building operation and maintenance stage, it addresses issues of operation and maintenance of building systems and processes, monitoring and recording of consumption, and occupant health and well-being, along with issues that affect the global and local environment.

GRIHA has been adopted by the Ministry of New and Renewable Energy (MNRE), Government of India, as an evaluation tool for measuring and rating a building's environmental performance. The ministry encourages construction of energy-efficient buildings through a combination of financial and promotional incentives based on their performance under the National Rating System to reduce consumption of electricity and other fossil fuels, in addition to having peak load savings in cities and towns.

REAPING THE BENEFITS OF GREEN

Sheila Sheridan, vice-chair of the U.S. Green Building Council's committee on LEED-EB, sums up her own definition of sustainability as "doing a little at a time and eventually making a difference." For Sheridan, who played a part in several pioneering green initiatives in her former role as director of facilities at Harvard University's John F. Kennedy School of Government, this incremental approach is ultimately an important part of what LEED is about, Sheridan is pragmatic about what will ultimately drive broader adoption of sustainability programs. While educational programs targeted at the public, property owners and vendors will have a slow but steady impact over time; the buyers and suppliers within the building industry need to see the return on investment for sustainability practices to become prevalent.

Those returns are becoming more tangible for many organizations today, which are increasingly taking advantage of government incentives/utility rebate programs and purchasing the growing number of products and services that support green initiatives. These incentives/rebate programs are well established in the United States and Europe and are now being implemented in India. The movement toward mainstream adoption of sustainable building practices is reflected in the growth of this market. In 2005, green building products and services in the United States represented a $7 billion market. This year, the total market value is expected to increase to $12 billion. Evidence of market adoption is similarly seen in the growth of USGBC's membership, which has quadrupled in the past five years, to include over 8,000 organizations.

What benefits do organizations expect from pursuing LEED certification for their existing buildings? The LEED-EB process, which allows an organization to measure, document, and benchmark its sustainability efforts, makes organizations aware of their responsibility toward sustainability, particularly the energy component. That's extremely important when you consider that the US Environmental Protection Agency (EPA) estimates that if every office building in the United States reduced its energy use by 30 percent, the resulting savings would be $30 billion a year. According to the US Department of Energy, just by employing currently available energy-efficient technologies, one can cut the cost of heating, cooling, and lighting their homes and workplaces by up to 80 percent. What could your organization do with such savings? Improving profit margins, increasing funds available for development of new products and services, and enhancing the overall corporate value are a few possibilities.

Quantitatively, Sheridan reports that LEED-EB certified properties extend the longevity of a building by 2.6 years, with an annual net savings of $170,000 when combined with best business practices.

Studies have shown that sustainable building practices also enhance employee productivity, as a healthier workplace leads to healthier employees, translating to less absenteeism, greater retention, and improved productivity.

The achievement of LEED-EB certification may be a long-term goal for many organizations. The amount of time it takes for an organization to achieve the required benchmarks and accrue enough points for certification varies, generally ranging anywhere from 6 to 18 months. But the review of sustainability practices and benchmarking of performance can in itself identify significant potential cost savings related to energy consumption and waste for most organizations.

Since energy represents the largest operational expense for most facilities—30 percent for a typical office building—an assessment of current energy usage and efficiency is a starting point for many organizations on the road to enhancing building sustainability. Given the volatility in energy prices, energy conservation measures and the resulting savings are of particular interest. The results of an energy assessment can lead to the identification of a variety of programs to reduce energy consumption in both the short and long term. These programs may range from the installation of more efficient fluorescent bulbs to the retrofitting of equipment that takes advantage of new technologies to heat or cool facilities more efficiently. Energy utilization for air conditioning can be optimized by strategies for proper selection and maintenance of AC equipment, capacity utilization and part-load operation management, timers, and automatic control valves for chilled water lines. Lighting savings involve voltage optimization, occupancy sensors, timers, energy-efficient lights, and reflectors.

Organizations can take advantage of significant rebates from their local utility provider when installing such equipment. These rebates are not only limited to heating, ventilating, and air conditioning (HVAC) equipment, however. Some utilities also offer rebates for companies replacing computer servers with newer models that employ more power-efficient processors.

Programs may also take the form of other improvements that are not part of a targeted energy program. Examples include increasing day-lighting in the course of a remodeling to cost-effectively introduce more energy-efficient design, or retro-commissioning a building, resulting in energy savings due to operational corrections.

By implementing practices and systems that help reduce energy costs, organizations can also take advantage of tax savings. In the United States, Energy Star programs currently enable owners or designers of new or existing commercial buildings to take a tax deduction of up to $1.80 per square foot if they save at least 50 percent of the heating and cooling energy of a building that meets American

Society of Heating, Refrigerating and Air-Conditioning Engineers (ASHRAE) standards for energy-efficient design. Partial deductions can be taken for measures affecting the building envelope, lighting, and heating/cooling systems.

In India, TERI has conducted hundreds of energy audits and has found savings of 5–25 percent of the annual energy bill. Payback for the recommended changes is typically less than three years. A large portion of these savings are from the AC systems; the remainder from areas like lighting. Recycling and green cleaning—using eco-friendly products for cleaning or hiring maintenance firms that employ green cleaning practices—are other areas where it is easy to make an immediate impact. Environmentally preferable purchasing generally improves worker safety and health and reduces related health liabilities, while diminishing health and disposal costs. These products are increasingly becoming comparable to their less environment-friendly counterparts in effectiveness and cost.

For those ready to take a broader view of their facilities' environmental footprint, carbon trading programs, which assign a dollar value to carbon dioxide emissions, are available in some regions to help curb the growth in greenhouse gases. In the United States, states such as California have rolled out programs for trading emission credits to promote "carbon neutrality."

The progress of green building initiatives is becoming increasingly evident and generating more interest by the day. Once gaining only marginal attention in mainstream building circles, sustainable facilities are becoming a growing reality for many forward-thinking organizations. This trend is evident in the manufacturing and corporate sectors as well as in government and higher education. Businesses are discovering that being a good corporate citizen embraces all of their resources, not just the financial bottom line or how "green" their products are. Schools and universities, for their part, are becoming more interested in making sure that their facilities and campuses reflect good stewardship and environmentally conscious building practices. In addition, both state and federal governments are also now taking sustainability seriously; for example, the US government now requires that all new federal constructions meet sustainability standards set forth under guidelines for LEED, requiring a minimum level of LEED Silver certification for public buildings that are larger than 5,000 square feet. Making these buildings more sustainable is a critical element to pursuing large-scale environmental benefits. Fortunately, sustainability initiatives in existing buildings also promote significant business benefits for organizations, ranging from enhanced employee productivity to operational savings. But how can an organization effectively evaluate its many sustainability investment options and focus its "green" dollars where they will have the greatest impact?

THE FIVE AREAS OF GREEN ASSESSMENT

The first step in identifying the best investment strategy for sustainability is an objective evaluation of an organization's current state of sustainability and its options for change, including estimated costs and potential benefits. Using the LEED®-EB standard, organizations can address the key categories of energy efficiency, water conservation, indoor air and environmental quality, materials and construction, and site sustainability.

Examining all these areas holistically—ideally within the context of overall facility improvement needs—can allow organizations to realize economies of scale and to bundle resulting projects cost effectively. However, for organizations looking to roll out green programs incrementally, the initial focus is often on energy efficiency, since more effective energy use can deliver the greatest cost savings. An evaluation of energy performance, including electrical and mechanical systems and the potential for renewable energy sources, should target recommended actions to reduce operating and consumption costs and decrease emissions. Such actions may take the form of installing lighting controls and energy-efficient lights or retro-commissioning a building's HVAC system.

With water costs rising in many municipalities, water consumption and treatment and the impact on discharge systems and water use practices should also be assessed to identify opportunities to increase efficiency, reduce waste, and support enhanced conservation, recycling, and reuse of water. The installation of water flow controls on faucet and flush systems or the capture of rainwater and distribution to landscaping for irrigation are some examples of water-saving initiatives.

Indoor air quality, lighting quality, and thermal comfort are also important elements of building sustainability. Enough fresh air provided through the building HVAC system is important to the health of building occupants. Reducing the use of materials or processes that emit toxic fumes is also important to air quality and occupant health. Eliminating ozone depleting gases from HVAC, refrigeration, and fire-suppression systems is critical to the integrity of the atmosphere. Enhanced day-lighting can also provide the joint benefits of decreased energy use and enhanced productivity for those who work in the affected area.

Materials and construction is another area where organizations may find short-term savings opportunities from green investments. Such savings can often be realized by reducing waste associated with building operations and maintenance, for example, through recycling and conservation programs and enhanced waste management practices. An analysis of cleaning products can also reveal options for more environmentally friendly options that promote greater environmental safety. The availability of construction materials that have recycled content or that are harvested from sustainable sources is growing significantly, and products such as flooring, wood products, furniture systems, structural steel components, or roofing materials can be increasingly obtained at prices equitable to their traditional counterparts.

Finally, organizations can identify opportunities for promoting a more sustainable building site by assessing ways to employ exterior lighting more effectively, alter landscaping to promote native species and reduce erosion, and make better use of storm water runoff. Transportation alternatives to and from the site can also provide opportunities for reducing energy usage and pollution. The reduction or protection of large surface masses such as parking lots and roofing systems that absorb and concentrate large amounts of heat and affect a site's microclimate is also important.

INTEGRATING SUSTAINABILITY PROGRAMS INTO THE CAPITAL PLANNING PROCESS

With detailed information about the costs and benefits of potential green investments, organizations can effectively evaluate which initiatives will ultimately provide the greatest results over the short and long term. Based on its overall business goals, each organization will have different values and therefore different strategies. For example, one organization may focus on investments that will deliver the greatest improvements to the quality of the work environment, while another may make its top priority those that provide operational cost savings or most significantly reduce environmental impact.

The many potential greening initiatives an organization can undertake compete with a myriad of other capital and operational investments—for systems renewal, building renovations, and new construction. Therefore, while organizations may single out opportunities to improve building sustainability for analysis, ultimately those investments will need to be assessed in the context of other building requirements.

Organizations that are early in the process of integrating green programs into their capital plans may choose to focus initially on relatively low-cost initiatives that can deliver short-term paybacks by reducing energy and natural resource consumption, prioritized based on cost savings and other desired benefits. As they make progress—and see results—they may go on to evaluate greening opportunities that can provide both short- and long-term environmental, social, and economic benefits. Such assessments may be conducted, for example, in support of major building renovations, large-scale master planning programs, or the acquisition of a long-term property holding. By combining this information with detailed data about overall requirements across a building portfolio, organizations can get a holistic view of facility needs, allowing them to maximize operational efficiency while promoting a sustainable built environment.

A LEADING EXAMPLE

The "2007 Kiwi Green College Report" names the top 50 schools that "will help your kids help the planet," and Salem State College, located in Salem, Massachusetts, was one of those 50 schools. The college has shown leadership by undertaking a groundbreaking approach to tracking sustainability on campus, and specifically focusing on its existing building stock. Stephen Keyes, Director of Campus Development, along with Thomas Osborne, Director of Sustainability, saw the value in combining their traditional facility condition assessments with green initiatives to meet the American College & University Presidents' Climate Commitment. VFA, Inc., the leading global provider of software and services for facility capital planning and sustainability, conducted facility condition and green assessments for Salem State College to establish a sustainability baseline which would serve as the foundation for a comprehensive green implementation plan. VFA has served over 400 organizations in the corporate, education, government, and health care markets.

Although funding wasn't currently being set aside for specific green initiatives, the need to be prepared to single out both projects and costs which could positively impact the sustainability of the campus was critical. As Mr. Keyes remarked, "We have positioned ourselves to be first in line when the funding becomes available and the best way to accomplish that was to know where we stand currently, what we want to undertake and how much it will cost."

Working with their existing facilities group and the outside consulting team who already provided their traditional assessment services, Salem State contracted a specially trained "green assessment" team to identify potential green opportunities and conventional operations and maintenance needs simultaneously. This allowed them to minimize the deployment costs and maximize the resulting data for the purposes of both meeting their conventional capital funding and planning goals and meeting their sustainability goals.

By working on one portion of their existing building portfolio at a time, they have been able to minimize the upfront investment and maximize the effectiveness of the dollars spent with a better decision-making process. As Salem State conducts assessments on buildings in the future, they will be able to apply the learning from the foundation provided by the green assessment. When the funding becomes available, they will be prepared to implement the projects which will improve the sustainability of their campus while advancing toward meeting the goals of the Climate Commitment.

GREEN IS GOLD

Ultimately, sustainable practices need to be integrated into both the facility management programs that organizations implement on a day-to-day basis, as well as into their long-term capital planning process. Facility managers today are on the frontline of this process, and positioned to raise the visibility and acceptance of these practices throughout their organizations.

As such, sustainable practices increasingly make good business sense; organizations will drive rapid market adoption, of which we are only seeing the leading edge today. This more holistic and socially responsible approach to facilities management will ultimately make the jobs of facility managers more critical for their organizations, as well as for future generations.

By evaluating sustainability opportunities—including those related to energy usage, environmental impact, and indoor environmental quality—and planning recapitalization with sustainability as a priority, corporate real estate and facility managers worldwide can be heroes—making improvements that will not only improve the financial value of their real estate portfolio today, but also help to save the planet, one building at a time.

RELATED WEB LINKS

The U.S. Green Buildings Council offers a LEED-EB Reference Guide which lists all criteria for certification: http://www.usgbc.org/DisplayPage.aspx?CMSPageID=174&#ebrg

IFMA's Green Zone features the white paper "Deliver the Green," which includes a discussion of the economic and operational benefits of sustainable practices for existing buildings: http://www.ifmafoundation.org/deliverthegreen.pdf

Cleaning Equipment, Accessories, Janitorial Supplies, Cleaning Chemicals and Sorbents, a catalog prepared by the U.S. General Services Administration, compares the environmental attributes of cleaning products: http://www.gsa.gov/gsa/cm_attachments/GSA_BASIC/sch79ib_R2H73-l_0Z5RDZ-i34K-pR.pdf

The Energy Research Institute: http://www.teriin.org.

Indian Green Building Council: http://www.igbc.in.

CHAPTER 11

Developing Green Innovation: DeCopier Paper Cleaning Products

Sushil Bhatia

This chapter presents a case that looks beyond the obvious in developing green innovation. Most people react to the current issues like green and sustainable products without investing the time in thinking outside the box. For example, they will attempt to reduce waste at home or in the office environment by using both sides of a piece of paper, or in many cases not printing at all. Also they will recycle their containers, boxes, and packaging. Unfortunately, most of these efforts are only temporary fixes since they are not always convenient and are not holistic solutions. More importantly, they do not offer substantial economic benefits to the end user. Therefore, it is necessary to find solutions which are easy to use, do not require a big change on the part of the end user and provide tangible benefits. In this chapter, I will describe the detailed development of a green innovation that overcomes the shortcomings of temporary, inconvenient solutions—a DeCopier.

A DeCopier works in a manner which is the exact opposite of a photocopy machine. In a copy machine clean paper enters at one end and then comes out with an image on the other side. In a DeCopier, a used piece of paper that is not needed any more enters the DeCopier at one end and comes out "clean" and reusable at the other end.

This is important since despite the heralded advance of the "paperless office" businesses are using more paper than ever in a trend that is expected to rise. Over the preceding two decades, the increased availability of photocopiers, fax machines, computer printers, and e-mail has resulted in a dramatic increase in the use of office paper. Americans alone consume more paper than do the citizens of any other country. According to the Association of Records Managers and Administrators, 95 percent of all information is recorded on paper, 46 percent of which (over 2.8 trillion sheets of paper) is used in laser printers and photocopiers.

The US per capita use of paper is nearly 600 pounds, approximately 1.61 pounds per person per day, 54 percent of which is white sheet paper (Interview North Shore Recycled Fibers, 1996). In spite of the electronic age the consumption of paper is projected to keep on increasing and by 2010 it is projected to reach over 16 million tons (Appendix 11A). At the same time the growth in printers is projected to grow as well (Appendix 11B).

Increased paper consumption has also led to an increase in the amount of confidential (classified and proprietary) information that is printed on paper. In commercial markets such as banks and high technology organizations, companies have been known to discard documents with names, addresses, phone numbers, social security numbers, patent drafts, and proprietary research. Research by the American Society for Industrial Security suggested a direct link between the increase in the use of paper and an increase in industrial espionage. The question is how to safeguard this classified and/or proprietary information and, more specifically, how to effectively destroy this material once it served the purpose for which it is generated. An entire industry has been created to address the destruction of confidential information and data destruction resulting in the growth of market for shredders (Appendix 11B).

The Security Industry Association stressed the vulnerability of confidential information on paper as a major concern for government and industrial users as early as 1998. This concern is also evident from the booming shredder market. Addressing the security issues of paper documents is the focus of DeCopier Technologies, Inc.

It is observed that printed information on paper, if improperly used, can compromise the value and security of the source. Conventional means of dealing with the removal of secure information such as incineration, shredding, and disintegration, focused on paper destruction, not information removal. The processes are noisy, dusty, and environmentally unfriendly. Even more important, they do not completely remove the information.

THE INDUSTRY

The document security industry has evolved from the use of incinerators to burn confidential printed information to the use of shredders, disintegrators, and pulping machines. In 2007, US government and businesses annually spent in excess of a billion dollars on document destruction equipment, primarily shredders and disintegrators.

In 1993, the National Industrial Security Program was established to safeguard classified information and to preserve US economic and technological interests. The Secretary of Defense, in consultation with all affected agencies and with the concurrence of the Secretary of Energy, the Nuclear Regulatory Commission, and the Director of Central Intelligence issued and maintained a National Industrial Security Program Operating Manual (NISPOM). NISPOM established consistent security policies and practices that are implemented throughout government and industry. NISPOM set forth methods for the destruction of classified information printed on paper, including shredding, pulping, and/or burning. The guidelines, for example, stated:

Classified documents should be destroyed as soon as practical. Pending destruction, classified documents shall be safeguarded as required for the level of classified material involved. Receptacles utilized to accumulate classified document shall be clearly identified as containing classified material. Once removed from a cleared facility for destruction, classified information shall be destroyed on the same day that it is removed.

For destruction of TOP SECRET material, two witnesses are re-quired. For destruction of SECRET and CONFIDENTIAL material one witness is required.

Destruction records are required for TOP SECRET material. The records shall indicate the date of destruction, identify the material destroyed, and be signed by the individuals designated to destroy and witness the destruction. Destruction records must be maintained for a period of 2–3 years.

Users of secure documents employ variations in the methods. However, none of these current methods of document destruction are considered 100 percent effective. Confidential documents are often lost in transit and interested parties have been known to hire people to reassemble shredded pieces back together. Most importantly, in highly secure venues, documents have to be disposed of on-site, creating a myriad of operational and safety challenges. Shredders create dust and noise, and disintegrators and smashing machines could be dangerous to operate. In high security organizations there are concerns about the elongated and multi-step processes necessary to destroy a document.

ADVANTAGES/DISADVANTAGES OF CURRENT METHODS OF DOCUMENT DESTRUCTION

Incineration, pulping, shredding, and disintegration are some methods of document destruction. They carried certain disadvantages. A brief synopsis of the existing technologies is included in the Appendix 11C.

Today, information elimination is handled by shredding, incineration, pulping, and disintegration. None of these current methods are 100 percent effective. Shredders must be repurchased every five years, require numerous hours to deploy, and create dust and noise in the process. In highly secure venues, it is preferable to dispose of documents on-site, creating with today's methodology, a myriad of operational and safety challenges. Other processes used today are slow, messy, toxic, and environmentally hazardous. All are wasteful. The issues of the elimination of confidential information set the challenge for the development of a more effective and efficient process—a process that simply removes the information (the toner) from printed documents produced by printers and copiers.

The innovation and proposed effort presented here relates to the decoying and reuse of office photocopy/laser-printed sheets. This concept will reduce the amount of paper waste that is disposed of by incineration or landfill, or reduce the hazardous waste and emissions of typical paper recycling operations. DeCopier Technologies' process for decopying laser-copied paper is simple and conducted at low temperature. The paper is wetted with a decopying fluid that is environmentally safe and can be recycled; the fluid releases the bond between the paper and the toner, lifting it off the paper, which allows the toner to be mechanically removed. The wet paper can then be dried and calendared to return to its original condition. The decopying process creates no waste streams that must be disposed of because the decopying fluid can be recycled within the decopying machine, and collected toner can be used in road surfacing materials.

Ultimately, the decopying process can be employed in office machines that will be capable of decopying paper and returning it in a state suitable for reuse. Automated decopying machines could process classified and confidential documents, providing greater security than tearing or shredding. Decopying fluids themselves have application in waste paper recycling where they offer an environmentally acceptable and lower cost alternative to present bulk decopying processes.

REMOVING TONER FROM COPY PAPER FOR WASTE REDUCTION AND INFORMATION PROTECTION

Printing inks are generally classified as impact and non-impact inks. Impact inks are used in conventional printing processes. These include letterpress, flexography, and lithography. Impact inks are composed of carbon black or a dye and are either water based or solvent based. They are pressed onto the surface of the paper, but do not fuse with it. The paper industry has very little trouble deinking impact inks paper.

Non-impact inks (toner) are composed of carbon black, pigments, and resins, which are bonding agents. Resins are cross-linked thermoplastic polymers; they fuse the pigments into the paper and into one another. This type of bonding makes the ink very difficult to remove in a de-inking process, because the polymers used in the binding reaction are highly resistant to chemical and mechanical action. Consequently, few paper recycling mills use laser ink waste ink paper. Furthermore, it constitutes 24 percent by weight and 40 percent by volume of all domestic and industrial waste in the United States. The adverse effects of large quantities of paper in landfill and incinerators cannot be overemphasized. However, it is important to emphasize the impact on forests. More and more wood is being consumed because most laser ink aster paper cannot be recycled. Increased use of this paper will greatly improve forest conservation.

DECOPIER TECHNOLOGY

DeCopier Technologies patented the solution chemistry and removal process by physically releasing the bond between the toner-based prints and paper through the use of a non-toxic, environmentally safe fluid system. It transported the particles from the surface and totally eliminated the original information. The process of removing toner is thus reduced to a repetitive and semi-automatic prototype unit.

The issues of the destruction of secure information outlined earlier set the challenge for the development of a better method for the removal of toner-based printed information generated in printers and copiers.

The award-winning patented decopying process involves the application of proprietary, non-toxic formulations to a sheet of paper. The process releases the bond between the printed toner and the paper. The particles are then mechanically transported from the sheet to a recycling chamber.

Sheets can be decopied, recopied/reprinted up to five times with no significant signs of degeneration.

The DeCopier technology, originally formulated to decopy toner from paper, has a number of other applications. These applications are extended to include confidential and classified information on sheets of paper, decopying overhead transparency film, decopying Mylar sheets used for utility engineering plans and blue prints.

TRANSPARENCIES

Overhead transparencies are used by large and small companies, students and professors to make colorful presentations. Some of the information being presented could be confidential in nature (market and financial information, research, and new product ideas). With the introduction of myriad software presentation programs like Microsoft PowerPoint, it is expected that the use of transparencies would decline. However, the opposite occurred— increasingly, people printed back-up transparencies for their presentations. Once the presentation is done, the imaged transparencies presented a significant disposal problem. The 3M Company, a major manufacturer of transparency film, projected that the US transparency market would be over 940 million sheets in 2010. It is also estimated that approximately 750 million sheets of transparency film (83 percent of what is sold annually) would be dumped into US landfills. This is equivalent to 15 million pounds or 6,800 tons of polyester, enough to wrap more than five times around the earth's equator every year.

Transparency film is considerably more expensive than a sheet of paper. Prices per new transparency sheet ranged from approximately $0.30 to $1.26 depending on the features the user needed. Assuming the purchase price for transparencies at the low end of the range, the annual cost to companies, universities, and individuals for purchasing those transparency sheets, not including the costs associated with dumping them into landfill, is over $225 million.

The process for decopying transparencies is slightly different than the process used for paper, due primarily to the nature of the transparency substrate materials. As the DeCopier technology and DeCopier machines evolved, it is planned that there would be DeCopier machines available for decopying both transparencies and paper. The transparencies could be reused and, because of the value of the base material, there is anticipated significant reuse in this market segment.

COST SAVINGS AND COST REDUCTION

The focus on protecting the disposal of intellectual property and other classified information would save customers a significant portion of expenses currently incurred in purchasing new paper, recycling and/or landfill charges, and document. This technology will have a long-term beneficial impact on the entire environment: saving trees, the atmosphere, animal habitats, and landfill space.

The information revolution multiplied rather than replaced paper use. According to the International Institute for Environment and Development (IDED), paper use has trebled during the last 30 years and could double again by 2010. According to research conducted by Giga Information Group, Inc., International Data Corp., and Dataquest, Inc., the number of sheets of paper consumed in US offices is going up 20 percent each year and is expected to hit 9 trillion sheets by the year 2010. When e-mail is introduced to an office, printing skyrockets by 40 percent (Narisetti, 1998).

Furthermore, it is estimated by the American Society for Industrial Security and the National Counterintelligence Center that a majority of the potential losses from intellectual property theft occurred through the conveyance of information printed on paper. Current methods of confidential document destruction are not considered to be the most effective means of addressing the issue of security in organizations that produced highly sensitive documents. Both government and businesses are in search of a better method of maintaining the security of printed information.

The DeCopier technology provides a solution that addresses both the need to maintain security of confidential information and, ultimately, the need to decrease the generation of current and future waste.

¡THE ADVANTAGES OF THE DECOPIER

- DeCopier is expected to decopy waste office paper and ready it for immediate use. It will save time.
- Even if there is no need to reuse the paper, information contained in it can be erased before disposal. It is known that government, corporate, and personal secrets are stolen from trash containers. Even when the paper is shredded, it can be pieced back together. Thus, information security will be protected.
- DeCopier will not pollute since its chemical formulations are environmentally safe. Excess decopying fluid can be condensed and reused. Brushed off toner will be collected in a separate compartment and reused in other ways. Toner can be used as filler in road surfacing. Resultant chemical waste will be minimal, and disposal, if any, will be easy.
- DeCopier will conserve forest resources. In the repulping industry, fiber yield is just about 70 percent. In the DeCopier process no fiber is lost. The sheet of paper comes out whole.
- DeCopier can decopy and recopy the same sheet of paper several times before it starts to wear out.
- DeCopier will conserve energy since it will operate at relatively low temperatures and does not pulp fibers.

- DeCopier is convenient. Because of its small size, DeCopier can be installed in office buildings just like photocopiers.
- DeCopier will be easy to service. It will require no extra personnel. Used cartridges will be collected, cleaned, and reloaded by the manufacturer's agents.
- Costs are low. Savings from using fewer chemicals, less energy, less water, and having less waste to dispose make DeCopier more cost effective.

ANOTHER LOWER COST SUSTAINABLE APPROACH: NANO DECOPIER PAPER PULPER

The approach to lower the cost of maintaining information, reducing waste, and converting waste is being achieved through creation of Nano DeCopier Paper Pulper. Appendix 11D shows its application and how at the end of it all there is no waste.

FINALLY

Green innovations like the DeCopier are sustainable technologies. They are convenient, permanent solutions, can reduce waste, and can create an output which is reusable—producing cost savings. Looking at the development of DeCopier, one can learn that it is possible to develop green, sustainable, and commercially feasible products. This case also illustrates that it is possible to develop products which can meet multiple market needs and applications. DeCopier not only reduces the paper waste but also helps save confidential information, offering a dual advantage to the end user.

Most importantly, this case demonstrates why it is necessary to get potential customers involved in the development process early. Getting input from customers helps the product design improve rapidly. User input also helps avoid costly redesigns and features adjustments to the product to meet customer's needs. One should remember that in new product development the important adage is: "Develop Fast: Revise Cheap."

Lastly, green products must make a strong economic case to justify their development. They should not be developed on an emotional basis but must be based on solid market data, information, and potential.

APPENDIX 11A: MARKET TRENDS—PAPER

Office Paper Usage Forecast

A 1991 study by INFORM included a 1990 EPA report (EPA, 1990) on office paper waste projecting continually growing usage/waste to the year (Table 11A.1).

TABLE 11A.1 Office Paper Waste 1960–2010 (Projection)

	1960	1970	1980	1988	2000	2010
Tons (millions)	1.5	2.7	4.0	7.3	11.8	16.0
Percent total MSW	1.7%	2.2%	2.7%	4.1%	5.5%	6.4%

Source: US EPA, Characterization of Municipal Solid Waste in the United States: 1990 Update, June 1990.

A 2006 RISI marketing study projects flat or dropping production in office paper owing to increased reliance on online/electronic communication as well as changing office culture. Production of coated sheet and uncoated free sheet (sources for office paper) in the United States was 21.35 million tons in 2005 and is expected to be 21.29 million tons in 2010, that is, essentially unchanged.

In keeping with this study, a 2006 EPA municipal waste report (EPA, 2006) found steadily increasing paper/paperboard generation from 1960 to 2000 but essentially flat generation from 2000 to 2005 (Table 11A. 2).

TABLE 11A.2 Materials Generated in the Municipal Waste Stream, 1960 to 2005

Materials	1960	1970	1980	1990	2000	2003	2004	2005
	Thousands of Tons							
Paper and Paperboard	29,990	44,310	55,160	72,730	87,740	83,030	86,360	83,950

Source: EPA, 2006.

That study also found 6.58 million tons office paper generated in 2005, comparable to the 7.3 million tons in the 1988 study. Based on the latter two studies, we can expect office paper generation to stay essentially unchanged in 2010.

APPENDIX 11B: MARKET TRENDS—FORECAST FOR PAPER SHREDDERS

In a 2005 *USA Today* article (Fetterman, 2005), Steven Jacober, President of the School, Home and Office Products Association in Dayton, Ohio describes the booming shredder market. He characterizes the industry as generating $350 million/year in revenues and manifesting growth in the low double digits every year.

Data Destruction and Compliance Management Forecast

A 2005 IDC Insight article (IDC, 2006a) indicates that IT department spending on compliance management will exceed $20 billion in 2009, increasing at a 22 percent compound annual growth rate through the 2005–09 forecast period.

Printer Forecast

According to a 2006 IDC report (IDC, 2006b), the worldwide printer market will show a –3.7 percent Compound Annual Growth Rate

(CAGR) during the forecast period 2006–10, with the only growth areas occurring in the monochrome and color laser markets. The color laser market is assigned a +15 percent CAGR over the forecast period 2006–10. The study on inkjet printers suggests a drop in those units over the period 2005–10 from 27 million to 24 million.

APPENDIX 11C: DIFFERENT FORMS OF DATA DESTRUCTION

- Incineration is a process by which matter is thermally decomposed through oxidation. Although the burning process has a long history, it produces toxic environmental contaminants, including ash and waste water. Incineration is capital intensive—an incinerator facility could easily cost up to $5 million and faces increasingly more stringent regulatory pressures.
- Pulping transforms paper into a moist, slightly cohering mass from which new paper products can be made. Pulping is considered an effective method of destruction because the printed sheets of paper are rendered into unreadable sludge. The pulp could be processed into new paper products, creating less landfill. The disadvantages are that pulping is slow and messy, produces an offensive odor and is extremely rigorous in its environmental and process control.
- Disintegration utilizes very sharp blades to pulverize paper and force it through a mesh screen into 3/64 inch particles. Disintegration met NISPOM requirements but is expensive and noisy, requires a large amount of space and an air-evacuation system to capture the dust generated in the process, and needs extensive maintenance and repair to avoid blade damage and paper jams.
- Shredding is a commonly used method of document de-struction. The US shredder market is estimated to be growing at 10 percent plus every year. Shredders are available in a vari-ety of shapes and sizes. There are three broad categories of shredder types, namely, straight cut, cross-cut/particle-cut, and

high security. Straight-cut shredders cut paper into long strips, each from 5/64″ to 3/4″ wide. Cross-cut shredders cut paper both lengthwise and crosswise. Cross-cut shredders produced a systematic shred cut which is available in many different sizes. Particle-cut shredders produced a non-systematic cut. High security shredders produce waste that conforms to the Department of Defense specifications for shredding. Shred size of these machines is approximately 1/32″ by 7/16″.

APPENDIX 11D: NANO DECOPIER PRODUCT SHEET

Product Description

Nano DeCopier is a desk-top low-noise environment-friendly unit for document decopying and destruction of sensitive and confidential documents. It is easy to use and is an ideal alternative to noise-making and difficult-to-handle shredders.

DeCopying/Destruction Capability

Nano DeCopier reduces the paper to pulp after a three-minute cycle. The resulting document destruction is impossible to reverse.
The unit uses a non-toxic and "green" cleaning mixture.

Applications: The Nano DeCopier Paper Pulper unit can decopy and pulp items like paper, business cards, junk mail (even unopened), pamphlets, booklets, newspapers, thin magazines, and small booklets. It can pulp the equivalent of 225–50 sheets of paper. You do not need to remove staples or paper clips before decopying/pulping.

Output: The resulting output can be used for making items like packing peanuts, paper mache products, flower vases, fireplace logs, and arts and crafts items.

At the end of it all there is NO WASTE.

REFERENCES

Fetterman, Mindy. (2005) "Identity Theft, new law about to send shredding on a tear," *USA TODAY*, 14 January 2005.

IDC. (2006a) "Technology Marketing Spending and Resource Priorities for 2006," Report published by 13 March 2006.

———. (2006b) "Worldwide Printer 2006–2010 Forecast and Analysis," Report Published by IDC, 6 November 2006.

Interview North Shore Recycled Fibers. (1996) Interview at their location in Fitchburg, MA, USA.

Narisetti, Raju. (1998) "Paper Chase," Market Section, *The Wall Street Journal*, 12 May 1998. p. 1.

U.S. Environmental Protection Agency (EPA). (1990) "Characterization of Municipal Solid Waste in the United States: 1990," Update, June 1990 issued by Environmental Protection Agency, Washington, D.C. 20460, EPA report ref. EPA/530-SW-90-042.

U.S. Environmental Protection Agency (EPA) (2006) "Municipal Solid Waste Generation, Recycling, and Disposal in the United States: Facts and Figures for 2005," issued by Environmental Protection Agency, Solid Waste and Emergency Response (5306P) Washington, D.C. 20460, EPA report ref. EPA-530-F-06-039, Oct. 2006.

CHAPTER 12

New Beginnings in Age-old Philosophies

Preeta M. Banerjee and *Vanita Shastri*

The new ventures or "new beginnings" described in this book arise from a *current* need for social responsibility and environmental sustainability. However, social responsibility and environmental sustainability are age-old philosophies. Examples of social responsibility and environmental sustainability can be found, for instance, in Indian agriculture and husbandry. In Indian villages, for hundreds of years, clean fuel has came from cow dung patties or briquettes made of cow dung and thatch. In turn, cows were fed in a manner that did not deplete a particular area of vegetation. Houses were built of biodegradable materials like clay and thatch. Plates were made of banana leaves, cups were made of clay, and hands were used as utensils. During Indian feudalism, landlords (i.e., *zamindar*s, *jagir*s, *desmukh*s, *chowdhury*s) lent land and money to farmers akin to today's microfinance.

We need to remind ourselves of age-old philosophies in order to create a better future. This book has been essentially about examples of such entrepreneurs: global social entrepreneurs. One of the pioneers in the field of entrepreneurship, Schumpeter (1934: 68), defined the entrepreneur as an undertaker of new combinations. Entrepreneurs are innovators who implement change within markets through carrying out new combinations.

> As a rule, the new combinations must draw the necessary means of production from some old combinations ... The carrying out of new combinations means, therefore, simply the different employment of the economic system's existing supplies of productive means ... development consists primarily in employing existing resources in a different way, in doing new things with them.

New combinations can arise from: *(a)* a new good or a new quality of a good; *(b)* a new method of production; *(c)* a new market; *(d)* a new source of supply of raw materials or semi-manufactured goods; and *(e)* a new organization (Schumpeter, 1934). The entrepreneurs in the preceding chapters describe their own unique combinations. For example, Pingle (Chapter 6) writes of meeting a new market need, Soni (Chapter 10) writes of a new method of building, and Bhatia (Chapter 11) writes of a new product.

In creating or discovering new combinations in existing or new ventures, entrepreneurs must take on an inherent risk. Many new ventures fail. Therefore, wherever and whenever entrepreneurial endeavors arise—entrepreneurship is often extremely difficult. This book illustrates some of the difficulties faced and overcome by successful global social entrepreneurs. These case studies are an exceedingly beneficial way to learn about the development of entrepreneurial endeavors and characteristics of social entrepreneurs. From these cases, we can come to some conclusions regarding hard-to-answer questions, like "what is social entrepreneurship?", "what is sustainability?", and "what are drivers of change?"

WHAT IS SOCIAL ENTREPRENEURSHIP?

We can see from the preceding chapters that social entrepreneurship is the work of an individual (or a group of individuals) who recognizes a social problem and use entrepreneurial principles to organize, create, and manage a venture to make social change. Social entrepreneurship can be found anywhere in the ecosystem of established firms, business entrepreneurs, government organizations, and NGOs and non-profit organizations. As illustrated in the following matrix (Table 12.1), there is an essential difference between business entrepreneurship and social entrepreneurship—the fundamental role of profits.

TABLE 12.1 Alternative Models for Entrepreneurship

	Social	Business
Purpose for setting up the venture	To create social change	Earning profits
Profitability	Not primarily motivated by "profit-making" (Being "profitable" helps self-sustainability of the venture, and also works as a mechanism for self-monitoring)	Should make a profit
The meaning of wealth creation	Creation of the social and environmental capital	"Wealth" is same as profits

Source: Preeta M. Banerjee.

Whereas a business entrepreneur typically measures performance in terms of profit and return, a social entrepreneur assesses success in terms of the impact she has on society. The main aim of a social enterprise is to further its social and environmental goals. This need not be incompatible with making a profit. Historically, the term social entrepreneurship was first used in the literature for social change in the 1960s and 1970s. It came into widespread use in the 1980s and 1990s, promoted by Bill Drayton, the founder of Ashoka. This book has given you modern-day examples of social entrepreneurs and the issues they face.

WHAT IS SUSTAINABILITY?

The preceding chapters also illustrate that sustainability is a current concern of many social entrepreneurs given the environmental burden that our current consumption has put upon the earth's resources. Sustainability is about meeting the needs of the current generation without compromising the ability of future generations to meet their needs. The authors have highlighted how sustainability can be achieved through business models that are environment-friendly, efficient, and effective.

DRIVERS OF CHANGE

Just as business entrepreneurs change the face of business, social entrepreneurs act as the change agents for society, seizing opportunities others miss and improving systems, inventing new approaches, and creating solutions to change society for the better. While a business entrepreneur might create entirely new industries, a social entrepreneur comes up with new solutions to social problems and then implements them on a large scale. This is illustrated by the following Venn diagram (Figure 12.1).

In the past, we have tended to focus on economic responsibility, particularly to shareholders. As Milton Friedman posits, this is the main purpose of business. However, economic responsibility can be balanced and enhanced by environmental and ethical responsibility.

Environmental responsibility can be met by minimizing waste production, maximizing recycling, and ensuring proper handling and disposal of solid waste; maintaining soil health by controlling erosion and improving soil fertility; preserving natural habitats for native species and protection of biodiversity; minimizing use of chemical pest management inputs that impact human, animal, and environmental health; maximizing water use efficiency and eliminating the release of waste into water; minimizing release of

FIGURE 12.1 Nexus of Responsibilities

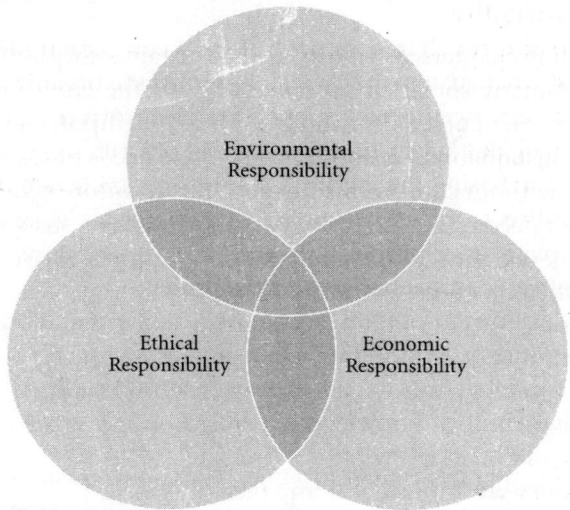

Source: Preeta M. Banerjee.

harmful by-products into the atmosphere; and maximizing energy-use efficiency and using ecologically sustainable renewable resources when feasible.

Ethical responsibility can be met by emphasizing a policy of integrity in the core values of the entrepreneurial endeavor. Also, it is important to ensure the health and safety of employees and the welfare and humane treatment of animals in the supply chain.

STARTING AND MAINTAINING SUSTAINABLE AND SOCIAL ORGANIZATIONS: LOOKING BEYOND ORGANIZATIONAL BOUNDARIES

The cases presented in this book show us that social entrepreneurship and sustainability in business is about looking beyond organizational boundaries to the ecosystem. Four main points can be learned from these cases.

- **Educate and communicate with the supply system about sustainability**
  It can be difficult to organize around a common understanding of what sustainability means within the organization, let alone work together with suppliers to move forward as a system. By laying out key responsibilities and priorities and ensuring that purchasing managers and suppliers are aware of them, the entire supply chain can be empowered to work together and make faster progress toward a common vision.
- **Develop a comprehensive global policy**
  Have policies to create a holistic perspective that will apply to all products purchased anywhere in the ecosystem and ensure that every link does its part to protect natural habitats. Develop mechanisms for knowledge to cross borders at the national, firm, and team levels.
- **Measure environmental impacts**
  Roll out an environmental scorecard to help identify the biggest impacts and opportunities for improvement in the areas of energy use, water use, air emissions, and waste production. Over 80 percent of Global Fortune 250 companies disclose their sustainability performance in "sustainability" or "corporate responsibility" reports. The most common standard is the G3 guidelines of the Global Reporting Initiative (GRI).
- **Foster a culture of creativity and innovation**
  The move to social impact and sustainability is not just about developing new alternative energy products but about recombining knowledge about being "smart" with existing technologies. Smart is an important word because it means three things: environment-friendly, efficient, and effective. Finding ways to make goods or provide services in a smart way involves every member of the ecosystem having an ability to be creative and innovative.

CONCLUSION

There are many takeaways that these cases provide for those interested in entrepreneurship that affects social change—social entrepreneurship. First, as to which social aspect one should tackle, we find that inspite of the many facets of social responsibility and sustainability, there are numerous individuals and organizations that can help us create our own goals and missions. Second, regarding drivers of change, each entrepreneur has her own drivers as illustrated in each chapter. Each chapter takes a different perspective (either from industry, entrepreneur, or non-profit), which facilitates the development of one's own unique drivers. Third, where do social entrepreneurs start? As the entrepreneurs showcased in this book have exemplified—just start! Last but not least, how does a social entrepreneur measure her success? The first two chapters help us to realize that though social entrepreneurs can use key performance indicators (KPIs) or other social impact measures, they are not myopic. Social entrepreneurs just think in broader terms. They focus on their venture's impact for the entire ecosystem. Organizations do not exist on an island! Social entrepreneurs need to partner with NGOs, corporations, government, and the community. The overall key conclusion of this book is that we need to build on our own personal capabilities and think out-of-the-box while constantly listening to current and future customers. It is extremely important to understand that customers are directly affected by social entrepreneurs—whether they be schoolchildren in India, women entrepreneurs in Africa, or businesses in the United States.

REFERENCE

Schumpeter, J. A. (1934) *The Theory of Economic Development.* Cambridge, MA: Harvard University Press.

About the Editors and Contributors

EDITORS

Preeta M. Banerjee is Assistant Professor of Strategy at the Brandeis International Business School. Preeta's research focuses on integration and cross-application of skills/knowledge across individuals, technology, the firm, the industry, and innovation ecosystem in the life sciences industries and clean technology. Since receiving her Ph.D. in 2006 from The Wharton School, University of Pennsylvania, Preeta has published and is quoted in several business and trade publications, including *R&D Management*, the *International Journal of Technoentrepreneurship*, *Business Week*, and the *Boston Business Journal*. She teaches MBA and undergraduate courses in competition and strategy, technology and strategy, and business and the environment. Prior to entering doctoral studies, Preeta spent close to three years at consultancy firms in the San Francisco Bay area working primarily with technology start-ups and received her B.S. in Computational Biology and Business Administration from Carnegie Mellon University.

Vanita Shastri is Executive Director, TiE-Boston. Shastri manages all TiE-Boston programs and works to lead the numerous activities and initiatives of the group. Vanita has been teaching business and entrepreneurship at Boston area colleges including Boston University's School of Management. She has also been a policy consultant at Harvard University, where she wrote a number of policy papers, including one on the "Software Policy of India" for the

171

Government of India. Vanita has worked for Redwood Investment Systems, Inc. in Boston where she led the effort to set up their wholly owned subsidiary in India and directed their global operations. Vanita has founded two non-profit organizations, including the Meru Education Foundation and the Habitat Learning Center in Delhi, India. Vanita is a trained Indian classical dancer and an active member of a number of civic organizations. She has a Ph.D. from Cornell University where she worked on India's industrial policy liberalization.

CONTRIBUTORS

Nishith Acharya is Executive Director, Deshpande Foundation. Nishith is on the board of the Akshaya Patra Foundation, and was previously Chief Executive Officer of Youth Tech Entrepreneurs. Nishith served five years as a presidential appointee in the Clinton administration with the administrator and deputy administrator of the Agency for International Development. Nishith also worked for Richard Riley on literacy initiatives and as associate director for the President's Office of Scheduling and Advance. Prior to that, Nishith was appointed to the Massachusetts Governor's Advisory Commission on Immigrants and Refugees. In the community, Nishith has served as president of the Boston Network of South Asian Professionals and on the boards of the Network of Indian Professionals of North America; the Indian American Leadership Initiative; the mayor of Boston School Readiness Project; LeadBoston; and the BU Global Health Initiative. Nishith has a Master's in Public Administration from George Washington University and a B.S. in Political Science from Northeastern University.

Meenakshi Verma Agrawal is the program officer for Global Exchange Programs at the Deshpande Foundation. After completing her degree, she was appointed to revitalize the Jamaica Plain Asthma Environmental Initiative, a struggling community-based, inner-city organization. She helped impact legislation, raised funds, and created a contractual relationship with a major HMO provider. In 2004, she moved to Mumbai, India for two years to work for the Alliance of Volunteers for Service, Action and Reform (AVSAR), a start-up non-profit focused on health care delivery to the slums of Mumbai. At AVSAR, she was in charge of organizing, fundraising, and managing the organization's infrastructure in India, and was responsible for over 65 successful experiences with volunteers from all over the world. She is active in organizations that follow issues of global public health and the Indian arts. Meenakshi received her B.Sc. and M.P.H. from University of Massachusetts, Amherst.

Sushil Bhatia is a globally known award-winning entrepreneur and innovator who has several patents, publications, and new products. Some products that he has innovated, developed, and has patents on are: Glue Stic, convention/seminar name badges, mailing labels, laser/copier labels, binding systems, decorative labels for shampoo/cosmetic/food containers, and a DeCopier. He has founded several companies and is currently the President and CEO of JMD Manufacturing Incorporated. He is also founder of the Laughing Clubs of America and has written *Just say "YES" to Laughing Your Way to Fitness with Yoga and Meditation (and that's no joke)*. His work has been featured on shows like ABC's Good Morning America, CNN, NBC, Canada AM, NPR, and has been written up in *The Wall Street Journal, Boston Globe, Economic Times*, and many other publications worldwide. Currently he is also a professor and executive in residence at Sawyer Business School, Suffolk University, Boston, where he teaches innovation and new product development.

Leona Christy is a program director at Pratham USA, the US-based fundraising arm of Pratham, established in August 2007. She manages day-to-day operations for the organization and oversees its fundraising efforts. Previously, she worked as a manager in sales and marketing at Hindustan Lever Ltd. (the Indian subsidiary of Unilever) for five years. In one of her roles as Key Account Manager, Leona was responsible for conceptualizing and setting up a new distribution channel targeted at large self-service stores. Leona has done her Masters in Public Policy and International Development from Duke University and has an MBA from the Indian Institute of Management, Bangalore. Her undergraduate degree in Economics is from St. Stephen's College, Delhi University.

Gururaj "Desh" Deshpande is co-founder and chairman of Sycamore Networks, Inc. Prior to co-founding Sycamore Networks, Dr Deshpande was founder and chairman of Cascade Communications Corp., which was acquired by Ascend Communications for $3.7 billion. Prior to Cascade, Dr Deshpande co-founded Coral Network Corporation in 1988 and served in various management positions for Codex Corporation, a subsidiary of Motorola. Before joining Codex, Dr Deshpande taught at Queens University in Kingston, Canada. Dr Deshpande holds a B.S. in Electrical Engineering from the Indian Institute of Technology, an M.E. in Electrical Engineering from the University of New Brunswick in Canada, and a Ph.D. in Data Communications from Queens University in Canada. Dr Deshpande has won numerous awards for his contributions to education and the greater community, and serves as a member of the MIT Corporation.

Vithal V. Deshpande graduated from Northeastern University, Massachusetts with a Master of Science Degree in Civil (Environmental) Engineering. Deshpande has multifaceted experience in engineering, management, policy, and regulatory aspects. His experience in public and private sector encompasses fields of sustainability, engineering, and management. Mr Deshpande's work in the field of sustainability has included development of greenhouse gas emission inventory, climate protection policy development, watershed management, public education for sustainability, comprehensive solid-waste management, environmental asset management, green building construction and education, energy management projects, zero pollution production process, zero-toxic polyester dyeing process, and multi-million dollars public construction project management.

Naveen Jha is director of the Deshpande Center for Social Entrepreneurship (DSCE) and manages the Deshpande Foundation's India operations. Naveen is engaged in building strategic collaborations with government, national, and local partners. Naveen is also founder and secretary of the TiE-Hubli chapter and also of a US-based non-profit organization called Action Exchange. Before joining the Deshpande Foundation, Naveen worked extensively on livelihoods, water resource management, food security, trade, and microfinance programs in India. Naveen worked with PRADAN, an Indian NGO, for six years. He also worked as a consultant to OXFAM America on South East Asia Regional Trade Policy while he was based in Cambodia. A recipient of the prestigious International Ford Foundation Fellowship (2005–07), Naveen completed his M.A. in International Development from Brandeis University. During his academic training years, he published seminal research papers in peer-reviewed journals on the subjects of food security and early childhood intervention.

Behzad J. Larry is a volunteer at American India Foundation (AIF) since November 2008. His interests lie in the fields of solid waste management and water conservation. His primary objective is to develop and implement environmentally friendly systems for the removal and processing of municipal waste in India. For the past year he has been researching within this field. He holds a bachelors degree in History and Classical Civilizations from Colby College.

Azad Oommen is the director of communications at AIF. He has been with AIF since 2003 and during that time, has held various leadership positions within the organization, overseeing the Service Corps Fellowship and developing a nationwide network of chapters. Previously, he has led the Clinton Democracy Fellowship at City Year in Boston and the Mickey Leland Hunger Fellows at the Congressional Hunger Center in Washington, D.C. He holds a Masters in Public Affairs from Princeton University.

Vibha Pingle is the president and founder of Ubuntu at Work, a non-profit focused on assisting women micro entrepreneurs in Africa and Asia. She has taught at Brown University, Harvard University, Rutgers, and the University of Notre Dame and has been a Fellow at the Institute of Development Studies in the United Kingdom. She has also been a consultant to the World Bank and other international organizations. She has also been a corporate consultant to Fidelity Investments.

Venkatesh "Venky" Raghavendra is the senior director of philanthropy at the American India Foundation. Prior to this, Venky worked in Washington D.C. with the global citizen sector organization "Ashoka: Innovators for the Public" leading Ashoka's "Global Diaspora Partnership" efforts. While at Ashoka, Venky also promoted social entrepreneurship in India and several other Asian countries. Earlier, in the late 1980s and early 1990s Venky co-founded an organization in the rainforests of South India to create livelihood opportunities for indigenous communities through eco-tourism and adventure-tourism.

Ameeta Soni is vice president, marketing and business development at VFA. She has been instrumental in the success of many new technology ventures. She was founder of Aanza AutoID Group, Aanza, and Altek Consulting. Previously, she held senior marketing positions at ChannelWave Software, Computer Identics, The BOC Group, Genus, and Varian Associates. Ameeta is a member of the board of directors of PlumChoice, Inc. She is past chair of the MIT Enterprise Forum of Cambridge, a charter member of TiE-Boston and an overseer at the Museum of Science, Boston. She serves on the Advisory Council for the College of Natural Sciences and Mathematics at the University of Massachusetts at Amherst. She has been published and quoted in several business and trade publications. Ameeta earned her MBA from the University of Chicago, M.S. from the University of Massachusetts at Amherst and B.S. (Honors) from St. Stephen's College, University of Delhi, India.

Vikas Taneja, a TiE charter member, is a partner and managing director with the Boston Consulting Group and a leader in BCG's

Technology, Media, and Telecommunication practice. While his commercial focus has been on driving turnarounds at major corporations, his social work is focused on education. Vikas is the Boston chapter leader and Executive Committee member of Pratham USA. He received his MBA with Honors in Economics & Finance from the University of Chicago. He also holds a Bachelor of Arts and Sciences in Computer Systems Engineering and Economic Development from Stanford University.

Daniel Wengrovitz is an economics major and Schiff Fellow at Brandeis University. His current research interests are entrepreneurship and innovation, with a focus on clean technology. While completing his undergraduate research project, Daniel attended the Clean Technology and Sustainable Industries Conference and Trade Show in Boston, Massachusetts where he found inspiration for much of his research. Prior to his research at the Brandeis International Business School, Daniel served as a summer financial analyst at Equity Residential in Wellesley, Massachusetts.

Duncan White leads the Science and Industry Business for Arup in the Americas. Duncan's role includes account management of major corporations in the science and industry sector, including Clarks, Procter and Gamble, Gillette, Intel, and Pfizer. As one of Arup's latest consulting offerings, Duncan has been supporting the development of Arup's management consulting offering focused around sustainability in the Americas. This includes the development of services around energy/resource management, the sustainable triple bottom line and preparing companies for the potential impacts of carbon management. Duncan's experience is global, having delivered major development projects in Europe, Africa, Asia, and the Americas. Duncan received his bachelors in Engineering from University of Bristol.

Steven F. Young is a senior vice president for consumer banking at Wainwright Bank and Trust Company, a publicly traded commercial bank founded in 1987 and headquartered in Boston with $1 billion in assets. Over the last three decades he has held a wide variety of positions within the banking industry and is currently the executive manager of marketing, public relations, and branding. Since 1992, Mr Young has collaborated with Wainwright Bank co-founder and co-chairman, Robert A. Glassman, in creating the bank's unique brand, recognized as one of the most socially progressive companies in the world.

Index